The Social Gospel in the South

The Social Gospel in the South

The Woman's Home Mission Movement in the
Methodist Episcopal Church, South, 1886–1939

John Patrick McDowell

Louisiana State University Press / *Baton Rouge and London*

Designer: Joanna Hill
Typeface: Goudy
Typesetter: G & S Typesetters
Printer: Thomson-Shore
Binder: John Dekker & Sons

Library of Congress Cataloging in Publication Data

McDowell, John Patrick.
   The social gospel in the South.

   Bibliography: p.
   Includes index.
   1. Methodist Episcopal Church, South—
Missions.   2. Women in missionary work.
3. Missions, Home.   4. Church and social
problems—Methodist Church.   5. Southern
States—Church history.   I. Title.
BV 2550.M27   266'.7633   82-15292
ISBN 0-8071-1022-1   AACR2

For Janet

Contents

Acknowledgments

A project like this requires the cooperation and assistance of many people. The staff of the Duke Divinity School Library, headed by Donn Michael Farris, frequently helped me in locating sources. Dorothy Ruth Parks of the Vanderbilt Divinity School Library facilitated my research by locating and providing me with copies of *Our Homes*. Emerson Ford of Perkins Library at Duke provided necessary assistance in the interlibrary loan arrangements. I am grateful also to the staffs of the Southern Historical Collection at the University of North Carolina, the Duke Manuscript Department, the Special Collections Department of Woodruff Library at Emory University, and the Archives Division of the Trevor Arnett Library at Atlanta University for their patient and instructive aid during my use of their facilities. To other librarians across the region who answered my queries, I also owe a debt of thanks.

I appreciate the help of others as well who have either read parts of the manuscript or listened to my ideas about my subject. They are really too numerous to mention by name. Special thanks, however, must go to Stuart Henry, Professor of American Christianity at Duke University, for his careful and critical reading of the manuscript. Robert Miller of the Department of History at the University of North Carolina also contributed substantially to my awareness of useful sources and to my ideas about my subject. I am particularly grateful also to Beverly Jarrett, Assistant Director and Executive Editor at LSU Press, and the staff of the Press, for their consistent support as I readied the manuscript for publication.

I wish also to acknowledge the assistance provided by a grant from Hollins College funded by the Mellon Foundation.

Finally, and most especially, I wish to thank my wife, Janet Dickey

McDowell. More than anyone else, she has made the completion of this project possible, providing insightful help with the formulation of ideas, the editing of copy, and the preparation of the manuscript. She has been a full and complete partner, a role that I think would be commended by the subjects of this book.

The Social Gospel in the South

Introduction

In his history of the Social Gospel, Charles H. Hopkins concludes that the social Christianity so prevalent in American Protestantism in the late nineteenth and early twentieth centuries was characterized by its emphasis on ethics and its stress on realizing the ideal of the kingdom of heaven in the world. Its proponents appreciated the effects of environment on human life and brought this idea to bear on their understanding of sin and redemption. They emphasized the role of social factors in creating sin and pointed to its corporate as well as personal nature. The redemption of this world and its social institutions assumed a place of importance alongside individual salvation. They shared the optimism of their age and believed that progress, though not inevitable, would come about through struggle against the entrenched forces of evil and economic exploitation. This conviction led them to criticize actively many of the basic tenets of capitalism.[1]

Hopkins focuses his attention on Protestantism in the East and Midwest and draws his conclusions primarily from the experience of these regions. He makes only brief reference to social reform efforts among southern Protestants, suggesting, at least through their omission, that such efforts were limited. Other historians of the Social Gospel during this period have conveyed a similar impression. Henry May, Aaron Abell, and Paul Carter have all provided accounts of American Protestantism's burgeoning concern with societal injustice and reform while virtually ignoring such activity among churches in the South.[2]

1. Charles H. Hopkins, *The Rise of the Social Gospel in American Protestantism, 1865–1915* (New Haven, 1940), 320–27.
2. *Ibid.*; Henry F. May, *Protestant Churches and Industrial America* (New York, 1949); Aaron I. Abell, *The Urban Impact on American Protestantism, 1865–1900* (Cambridge, Mass., 1943); Paul Allen Carter, *The Decline and Rise of the Social Gospel* (Ithaca, N.Y.,

Many of the region's most distinguished historians have also noted the apparent absence of social concern in its religious history. Samuel S. Hill, Jr., argues that the "central theme" of the area's theology for over a century has been its concern with individual salvation. Southern denominations, he notes, regard conversion as the church's primary task; he sees "virtually no recognition of any responsibility to redeem the secular dimensions of community and national life." Specifically, Hill suggests that social Christianity in the late nineteenth and early twentieth centuries "made only the slightest impact upon the churches in the South." Hill's sentiments are echoed by C. Vann Woodward. Writing of the early years of the twentieth century, Woodward contends that there is scant evidence of social concern among southern Protestants. "Instead," he maintains, "there is evidence that the current in the South ran counter" to that tendency.[3]

Recently, however, other historians have perceived greater evidence of social interest. Donald Mathews has demonstrated that in the antebellum South, blacks and women often heard the reforming message of the Christian gospel, with its emphasis on equality and liberty. Jacquelyn Hall has chronicled the important role churchwomen played in the antilynching campaign in the 1930s. There appears to be increasing support for the contention of John Eighmy "that much social thought in Southern religion which has been classified on the liberal side has been overlooked."[4]

This study contributes to the growing evidence that the history of southern Christians includes a concern for social reform. The focus is the

1956). Hopkins, it should be pointed out, does note the activities of the Southern Sociological Congress (pp. 278–79), whereas the others do not examine Social Gospel influence in the South.

3. Hill acknowledges the social concern of a limited number of denominational officials and clergy but fails to account for the more extensive involvement of church groups and church members as evidenced by many women in the Methodist Episcopal Church, South. Samuel S. Hill, Jr., "The South's Two Cultures," in Samuel S. Hill, Jr. (ed.), *Religion and the Solid South* (Nashville, 1972), 48–49; C. Vann Woodward, *Origins of the New South, 1877–1913* (2nd ed.; Baton Rouge, 1971), 450.

4. Donald G. Mathews, *Religion in the Old South* (Chicago, 1977); Jacquelyn Dowd Hall, *Revolt Against Chivalry: Jessie Daniel Ames and the Women's Campaign Against Lynching* (New York, 1979); John L. Eighmy, *Churches in Cultural Captivity: A History of the Social Attitudes of Southern Baptists* (Knoxville, 1972), 61 n.

organized home mission movement among women in the Methodist Episcopal Church, South. The women understood home mission work as Christian work that reached beyond the members of the local congregation and usually beyond members of the denomination. They distinguished it from foreign mission work, however, because it addressed problems and needs in the United States. The period under examination begins in 1886, when the women began their first denomination-wide home mission work, and ends in 1940, when the work came under the authority of the newly formed Methodist Church—a merger of the Methodist Episcopal Church, South, the Methodist Episcopal Church, and the Methodist Protestant Church.

Although the number of women involved in home mission work increased during the period being considered, they always remained a minority of the denomination's total female membership. The members of home mission societies grew from a few thousand to approximately sixty thousand just prior to the merger in 1910 of home and foreign mission societies. By 1940, the membership of the joint societies numbered approximately three hundred thousand in a denomination whose total membership was almost three million, a majority of whom were women.[5]

Although this study considers the broad range of home mission activities among these women in the Methodist Episcopal Church, South, it centers primarily on the opinions and efforts of women whose talent and energy brought them to positions of prominence in the denomination's home mission work. This leadership group usually held office in the missionary societies, wrote most frequently in the mission periodicals, and directed particular mission projects.

This study argues that a careful analysis of the organized home mission work undertaken by the women of Southern Methodism and of the religious ideas that informed and were informed by the work further dispels the notion that southern religion has manifested little or no concern with social reform. A thorough examination of the statements and activ-

5. Arabel W. Alexander, *Life and Work of Lucinda B. Helm* (Nashville, 1904), 69; Mary Helm, "Work for the Laywomen in the City," *Our Homes*, XVIII (January, 1909), 2; Bessie W. Lipscomb, "'God Thought of Us,'" *World Outlook*, XXX (August, 1940), 34; Edwin S. Gaustad, *Historical Atlas of Religion in America* (New York, 1962), 78.

ities of the women most active in home mission work in the MEC,S, reveals, on the contrary, extensive interest in a variety of social problems and widespread familiarity and contact with other American Protestants promoting a social gospel. For over half a century, the women showed a genuine concern for the nation's problems and the victims of those problems.

The women found inspiration for their work in a Methodist heritage that stressed ethical living and divinely aided human growth. This tradition provided religious impetus for them to undertake and continue the work. They were also aided by a society that, somewhat grudgingly, was making more opportunities available to women outside the home and by a denomination that gave their work considerable autonomy. In addition, they were deeply influenced by the words and deeds of a growing phalanx of socially concerned Protestants in their own day.

Sharing with this latter group the hope of extending God's kingdom on earth, the women were convinced that Christian missions should meet the physical and social as well as the spiritual needs of people. They challenged the viewpoint that religion should have little or no involvement with social issues. The women came increasingly to the conviction that all persons, because they were creatures of God, possessed inherent worth and the potential for useful, moral lives—though of course not all had achieved their full potential. In the course of their home mission work, the women became more and more aware of the influence of the social environment on all people's lives and lamented the harmful consequences of poor living conditions. Progress became contingent on reform; human effort in effecting social change was imperative.

During the more than half century of organized home mission work, the women's efforts were diverse and far-reaching. They showed particular concern for the home environment of immigrants, native poor whites, and blacks. They sought to eradicate conditions that they considered detrimental to family stability; they were especially concerned about the well-being of children. They supported Prohibition, counseled moral strictness, and criticized unsavory conditions. To their mission work among poor whites and blacks, they brought an attitude of concern that, though often mixed with condescension, nevertheless consistently sought for the recipients better education, updated medical care, improved living conditions, and other social improvements. In addition to these activities, they wholeheartedly supported the pursuit of world peace and continued their long-standing effort to secure an expanded role for women in their own denomination. A close examination of their work shows that religious ideas, especially the vision of extending the kingdom of God on earth, were a major factor in instigating and shaping their varied reform activities.

Chapter I / *Small Beginnings and Large Visions*

On May 7, 1886, the General Conference of the Methodist Episcopal Church, South, meeting in Richmond, Virginia, adopted a memorial from the denomination's Board of Church Extension establishing the Woman's Department of Church Extension in order to raise funds for building and repairing parsonages for ministers and their families doing mission work in the American West. Thus was begun the first church-wide woman's organization for promoting home missions in Southern Methodism.[1] Probably no one in the all-male group, which passed the memorial without prolonged debates or significant opposition, had any premonition of the eventual significance of what they were establishing. Two weeks later the Board of Church Extension elected Lucinda B. Helm general secretary of the new Woman's Department.[2]

Lucinda Helm already had a vision of the work churchwomen might do in this country. Born into a wealthy and politically prominent Kentucky family, she had from an early age preferred religious work to social activities. She taught Sunday school, carried charitable gifts to the poor, shared her religious ideas with the family servants, and organized religious clubs for local children. Although frequently in poor health, she found time and energy for church activities. She actively supported the growing assistance Southern Methodist women were giving foreign missionaries and applauded the establishment of the Woman's Foreign Missionary Society by the denomination's General Conference in 1878. Yet, she remained convinced that women also could play a much greater part in mission work in this country.

1. *Journal of the Tenth Session of the General Conference of the Methodist Episcopal Church, South* (Nashville, 1886), 127. *Southern Methodism* refers to the Methodist Episcopal Church, South. Similarly, *Southern Methodist women* refers to women of that denomination, especially those active in home missions.
2. "General Conference Proceedings," *Daily Christian Advocate*, XI (May 18, 1886), 2; *Fifth Annual Report of the Board of Church Extension* (Nashville, 1887), 58–59.

Soon after the Board of Church Extension was organized in 1882, she was asking its general secretary Dr. David Morton, a longtime friend, for a greater role for herself and other interested women. Her opportunity came in 1885. Bishop R. K. Hargrove returned from the West, lamenting that several pastorates had to be abandoned because there were no adequate houses. When the Woman's Foreign Missionary Society denied his request for aid because it could not undertake additional work, he turned to Morton.

Here was Lucinda Helm's opportunity. Her plan for the home mission work of women apparently extended well beyond parsonage assistance. It included charitable work and religious instruction among those in need of both. But in 1886 she could get little support to undertake this broader plan. She would not relinquish her vision, but she would take what she could get. In January, 1886, the Board of Church Extension accepted the plan she formulated for a Woman's Department; five months later the General Conference incorporated it, with minor modifications, into the constitution of the Methodist Episcopal Church, South.[3]

This modest beginning had roots in the work already undertaken by churchwomen. Throughout the nineteenth century, women in many leading Protestant denominations showed interest in foreign and home mission activities. Groups, both North and South, had from the beginning of the century aided missionaries already at work, in and out of the United States. Many churchwomen, most often in urban areas, also formed and joined organizations designed to do benevolent or religious work in their own localities.[4]

Methodist women were a part of this early work. Only in the final decades of the nineteenth century, however, did the home mission work rapidly expand. The Woman's Home Missionary Society of the Methodist Episcopal Church was formed in Cincinnati in July, 1880, and came

3. Alexander, *Life and Work of Lucinda Helm*, 13–65; "The General Work of the Woman's Home Mission Society: A Historical Sketch of Its Growth and Development," *Our Homes*, XIV (October, 1905), 1.
4. R. Pierce Beaver, *All Loves Excelling: American Protestant Women in World Mission* (Grand Rapids, 1968), 13–34; Anne C. Loveland, *Southern Evangelicals and the Social Order*, 1800–1860 (Baton Rouge, 1980), 167–71.

into relation with the General Conference of that church four years later. Its first president was Lucy Hayes, First Lady of the country, and one of its first major efforts was on behalf of free blacks in the South, particularly among women and girls. Some scattered efforts by these women on behalf of southern blacks predated the formation of the Home Missionary Society of the MEC, but during the 1880s the society expanded the work. In 1883 it established seven Bureaus of Information to obtain facts about problems in various areas and make suggestions about possible solutions. Among these bureaus was one for "Colored People in the South" and another for "Illiterate Whites in the South." Throughout the last years of the century, the society undertook efforts at aiding free blacks and, to a lesser extent, poor whites in the South. These efforts usually took the form of training for women in homemaking and other vocational skills as well as religious and moral training.[5]

Home and foreign missions began essentially as two parts of the same movement among women of the Methodist Episcopal Church, South. The first effort in the denomination to start missionary work among women began on the Lebanon Circuit in Bethlehem, Tennessee. As early as the 1830s, Mrs. M. L. Kelley, whose husband pastored the charge, was doing missionary work there and established a society at one of the churches on the circuit. There is no record of further activity until the late 1850s, when she rejuvenated the work in order to support the mission efforts of Mr. and Mrs. J. W. Lambuth in Shanghai, China. The advent of the Civil War ended this initial effort, but Kelley would not be thwarted. In the early 1870s, she again attempted to organize a missionary society, this time in McKendree Church, Nashville, Tennessee, where her son was pastor. Initially, her efforts bore little fruit. Finally in

5. During the 1870s, Mrs. Joseph Hartzell, later assisted by Mrs. M. A. Ryder, began visiting blacks in New Orleans, giving religious instruction and guidance in practical matters such as health and housekeeping. Although northern women would continue projects in the South into the twentieth century, these efforts were soon overshadowed by the efforts of the Southern Methodist women themselves. There seems to have been no antagonism between the women of the two denominations. In fact, they often exchanged delegates at their annual meetings and frequently borrowed program ideas from one another. Ruth Esther Meeker, *Six Decades of Service, 1880–1940: A History of the Woman's Home Missionary Society of the Methodist Episcopal Church* (Cincinnati, 1969), 4–7, 19, 24–25, 43, 78–80, 91–178.

April, 1874, after the proposed organization was extended to include other Methodist churches in the district, Kelley and her supporters organized the Woman's Bible Mission of Nashville. The purpose of the mission was not only to aid foreign missions but also to visit the sick and aid the poor and instruct them in the Scriptures. The major home mission project was to assist in founding a home for unwed mothers. Some men aided in the controversial project, but the women were the "pioneers of this charity."[6]

Mrs. M. L. Kelley was a persistent pioneer, but in the years just before and after the Civil War other women in other localities were showing increasing interest in missions, both foreign and home. Mississippi women in Natchez and Woodville also supported the China efforts of the Lambuths. In Baltimore, Southern and Northern Methodist women worked together on mission projects for the needy and the unchurched of the city; they also supported foreign projects. In February, 1869, several MEC,S, women there formed their own organization, the Trinity Bible Mission, to continue similar work.[7]

The growing interest in mission work among southern women in various places led eventually (1878) to the founding of the Woman's Board of Foreign Missions by the General Conference of the church. This action drew most of the women's efforts for the following few years toward foreign missions. Perceiving the vacuum that remained in home mission work, Laura Askew Haygood, with the encouragement of her pastor Dr. T. R. Kendall, formed the Trinity Home Mission in Atlanta in 1882 to improve the "physical, mental, and moral elevation of the poor of the city, and especially of . . . [the local] Church and congregation." Haygood had served as both teacher and principal at the Girls' High School in Atlanta. An extremely gifted teacher, she applied her talent to the church as well. Deeply involved in Southern Methodist work—her brother, Atticus, was a bishop of the denomination—she was convinced that women had not taken their rightful place in the missionary work of

6. John D. A. Autry, "History of the Woman's Missionary Council, Methodist Episcopal Church, South, 1910–1940" (B.D. thesis, Duke University, 1940), 13–19; R. K. Brown, *Life of Mrs. M. L. Kelley* (N.p., 1889), 101–106.
7. Brown, *Life of Kelley*, 73; Autry, "History of Woman's Missionary Council," 13–19.

the church, either in evangelism or in outreach to the poor. They, as well as men, needed to understand that they had a God-ordained role in the uplift of the downtrodden.[8]

At Trinity Mission, most of the work was done with black women and children, and, as was to be the case with most home mission efforts, it combined social and religious elements. Sewing lessons would be followed by Bible lessons, and practically all the women and children who came to the church for instruction or recreation came also for special worship services, segregated from the regular Trinity services. But two years later Laura Haygood would herself become a missionary to China. She had encouraged Georgia women to consider the formation of a society beyond the local church for home mission work, but her efforts met with little success. To Lucinda Helm went the responsibility of making the idea of a broader society a reality.[9]

Although there was much sentiment for limiting the activity of women, the times were propitious for women in the South, particularly the well-to-do, to take on an expanded role in their society. Many had assumed new responsibilities outside the home during the Civil War while their husbands were away, and many continued to do so after the war, especially since the male population of the region had been so reduced. In addition, the freed black population ensured that servants were still plentiful. Many of the wealthier women were left with considerable leisure time. Thus southern women began to seek increasing opportunities in education and vocations such as teaching, law, and journalism, but it was in the church that women found their greatest opportunity for service.[10]

Lucinda Helm envisioned such opportunities. She poured enormous energy into her new undertaking, and the results were quite remarkable. By 1888, 214 local home mission societies were formed, with over 3,500

8. O. E. Brown and Anna Muse Brown, *Life and Letters of Laura Askew Haygood* (Nashville, 1904), 89–94; Mabel Katherine Howell, *Women and the Kingdom: Fifty Years of Kingdom Building by the Women of the Methodist Episcopal Church, South, 1878–1928* (Nashville, 1928), 49.

9. Brown and Brown, *Life and Letters of Laura Haygood*, 71–74, 86–88.

10. Anne F. Scott, *The Southern Lady: From Pedestal to Politics, 1830–1930* (Chicago, 1970), 105–133.

members. Still she was not satisfied. She told members in a leaflet that she and other leaders were "restive under the fact that . . . [the work moved] more slowly than it should, because of the inactivity of those who should most vigorously push it on."[11] Despite poor health, she worked persistently. In the next two years, the number of societies and members almost doubled, and there was a dramatic increase in the number of parsonages aided.

Yet repairing and building parsonages was not enough for Lucinda Helm. She believed that the women of the church should be given a larger and more autonomous work. She was deeply concerned about "places where utter godliness mingled with a heathen element native to the soil and flowing in from foreign." She felt, and knew that other women must feel, the call "to Christianize these Barbarous and ungodly elements in the midst of a Christian civilization." Her plan was to reform non-Christians, native and foreign, bringing them into the mainstream of her country and her religion. Her biographer wrote that "nothing less than the fullest and completest organized effort for home missions could satisfy her."[12] She determined to make a plea at the 1890 General Conference for an enlargement of the work given to women.

Initially, she encountered opposition from women as well as from men who feared that broadening the work would undermine the parsonage work already being done and might interfere with foreign missions. She countered that an organized, active women's work for home missions would surely stimulate other phases of women's work in the church, as well as the work of the church as a whole. Her persistence and skill

11. Alexander, *Life and Work of Lucinda Helm*, 69,75. Helm's efforts on behalf of home missions were legendary. Francis Downs notes that Bishop H. C. Morrison wrote that never in the church's history had such "a great brain, sustained by so frail a body, accomplished through arduous toil such a work." Perhaps the most remarkable account was provided by Downs himself. "Sometimes forced to sit up all night long with ice packed around her heart to keep that frail organ from ceasing to beat, with a hundred burdens too heavy for her weak frame to bear, with a task that seemed too great for human hands, she sounded no note of retreat—she persevered till her work was done." Francis A. Downs, "The Greatest Woman in Southern Methodism," *Methodist Quarterly Review*, LXIV (April, 1915), 264; *Sixth Annual Report of the Board of Church Extension*, 31.

12. *Seventh Annual Report of the Woman's Parsonage and Home Mission Society of the Methodist Episcopal Church, South* (Nashville, 1893), 24–25; Alexander, *Life and Work of Lucinda Helm*, 80–81.

brought the victory. On the recommendation of certain key males, the General Conference amended the constitution so that the Woman's Department of the Board of Church Extension became the Woman's Parsonage and Home Mission Society, thus giving the organization a more independent status and broadening its powers to include not only collections for parsonages but also additional undertakings "otherwise aiding the cause of Christ."[13]

With this broadened authority, the women of Southern Methodism could undertake a range of home mission activities. The response was quick. Education for the poor or the unchurched was the first major project. In 1892 the Wolff Mission School was opened in Ybor City, Florida, for the children of Cuban immigrants, and two years later a similar project was undertaken in west Tampa. In 1896 the Sue Bennett Memorial School was begun in London, Kentucky, for the poor children of this mountain area, and in the same year the Industrial Home and School at Greeneville, Tennessee, opened for orphans. A year later night schools were begun for Chinese and Japanese on the Pacific Coast. These projects presaged considerable activity by the women in education during the half century to follow.[14]

In addition to educational work, the women soon became convinced of the need for home mission work in the cities. Increasing exposure to social problems convinced the leaders of the Parsonage and Home Mis-

13. Alexander, *Life and Work of Lucinda Helm*, 80–92; *Journal of the Eleventh Session of the General Conference*, 235–36. Although the new organization was largely autonomous, administration of parsonage funds remained under the control of the Board of Church Extension. Leadership was provided by an eleven-member Central Committee. In 1898 the General Conference granted the women's further request that the Woman's Parsonage and Home Mission Society be renamed the Woman's Home Mission Society of the Methodist Episcopal Church, South. In addition to being given a new name, the society was granted more representative leadership, with the Central Committee being replaced by the Woman's Board of Home Missions, which included general officers and representatives from each conference (*Journal of the Thirteenth Session of the General Conference*, 155–56). This organization continued until 1910, when the General Conference voted to merge the Woman's Board of Home Missions and the Woman's Board of Foreign Missions into the Woman's Missionary Council. The council survived further name changes until 1940. Noreen Dunn Tatum, *A Crown of Service: A Story of Woman's Work in the Methodist Episcopal Church, South, from 1878–1940* (Nashville, 1960), 28–34. *Board* and *council* are frequently used herein to designate the appropriate body. *Society* is used to refer to the general organization throughout its history.
14. "The General Work," 1–2.

sion Society that they should organize and expand the work among the urban poor, particularly among immigrants. As early as 1891, the Central Committee, which directed the Parsonage and Home Mission Society, determined to call a meeting of representatives of the society as well as other groups to consider the possibility of Christian workers in urban areas. The meeting was finally held in Saint Louis at Saint John's Methodist Episcopal Church, South, in May, 1893. The meeting marked the beginning of the women's organized city mission work.[15]

The tone for the meeting was set by Mrs. John Mathews, president of the Saint Louis Conference Society, in her welcoming address, when she emphasized the "gulf, a wide gulf, between the Church and the masses" and called on the women to undertake work among the unchurched. The work she foresaw was to address both physical and spiritual needs. She acknowledged the importance of providing "physical necessities" to the poor, but she reminded these churchwomen that their "efforts must not drop to the plane of an ordinary philanthropic organization, or an ethical society, or a sociological movement. The work must be more than philanthropic: it must be evangelical."[16]

Saint Louis was itself the first city to respond. Soon after the convention, the home mission auxiliaries in the city met and organized for work, employing Mrs. M. R. Skinner as a special worker. Soon thereafter a similar organization was created in Nashville, with Tina and Emma Tucker employed as city missionaries. Similar work soon began also in Atlanta, Houston, New Orleans, and Los Angeles. This organized work in the cities received further impetus in 1894, when the General Conference provided for the formation of city mission boards, composed of two members from each of the participating auxiliaries, to direct the work within a city.

Although varying somewhat between cities, the work itself was a mixture of social outreach and religious instruction. Skinner reported to the society that she established kindergartens and sewing schools, helped the sick obtain medical attention, and provided clothes and food for the

15. Sara Estelle Haskin, *Women and Missions in the Methodist Episcopal Church, South* (Nashville, 1925), 199–201.
16. "Convention of Christian Workers," *Our Homes*, II (June, 1893), 1.

poor. The Tucker sisters, while alleviating social needs, also involved themselves extensively in evangelical activities, conducting meetings for Bible reading and prayer during revival services and rejoicing in those who had professed their faith.[17]

To increase the work, however, the society's membership and the women of the denomination had to be informed about the work and educated to the need for further efforts. Leaflets explaining the work and discussing problems of interest to the women had from the beginning been widely distributed and would continue to be. Lucinda Helm reported in 1888 that she had already distributed 24,000 leaflets. Yet, as usual she believed that more must be done. She made plans to publish a periodical for the society. In January, 1892, the first issue of *Our Homes* appeared, with Helm as editor. Originally published quarterly and later monthly, it featured articles on various concerns germane to home missions and accounts of the work the women undertook. After the first year, it had approximately two thousand subscribers and remained vital to the organization until its merger with other mission publications in 1910.[18]

In 1894 the Central Committee decided to establish for the membership a course of reading materials pertinent to home mission work. Announcing this in *Our Homes*, Lily Hammond, who was herself the most prolific writer among the women, argued that if America was to remain a Christian nation, Americans must better understand their country—"its needs, its perils, its resources, as well as the work which other Christian people are doing in this and other lands for the cause . . . at heart." This daughter of slaveholders and wife of the white president of black Paine College was convinced that ignorance was the greatest stumbling block to social reform. The reading course was to provide better information to the women about how to go about home mission work, in its social and evangelical dimensions. "We want to know of everything," she wrote, "that is being done in all the world to uplift the fallen, to better the

17. Haskin, *Women and Missions*, 199–201; *Eighth Annual Report of the Woman's Parsonage and Home Mission Society*, 12–13.

18. Alexander, *Life and Work of Lucinda Helm*, 69; *Seventh Annual Report of the Woman's Parsonage and Home Mission Society*, 37. In 1910 *Our Homes*, the *Woman's Missionary Advocate* (a publication of the Woman's Foreign Missionary Society), and *Go Forward* (a pub-

condition of the poor, to bring classes together, to make straight paths for stumbling feet, whether the work be for the physical, mental, or spiritual betterment of those who need it." [19]

The first two books recommended were major treatises by leaders of the newly emerging social Christianity, Josiah Strong's *Our Country* and Washington Gladden's *Applied Christianity*. Authors listed through the years in addition to Strong and Gladden included Walter Rauschenbusch, Shailer Mathews, Charles Stelzle, and Richard Ely—all major representatives of the Social Gospel. Books concerned with social issues and their relation to the gospel, frequently written by important Social Gospel figures, dominated the list and influenced the women's thinking. [20]

These activities show that the beginning years of organized home mission work were years of growth. Yet there was also considerable opposition, from both men and women, to the efforts to expand the work. In her 1890 report to the Board of Church Extension, Lucinda Helm acknowledged that home mission work was suffering because of the effect many feared it would have on the foreign mission program. Women committed to the quite recently established work for foreign missions saw this new program as draining money and energy that should be used in their work. The new home mission society at the Mulberry Street Church in Macon, Georgia, was asked to disband by the women in the church active in foreign missions because they feared that the society would wreck the foreign mission enterprise. [21] Other local societies experienced similar opposition.

---

lication of the Board of Missions) were merged into a new periodical, the *Missionary Voice*. In 1932 the name was changed to *World Outlook* (Tatum, *Crown of Service*, 71–72).

19. Lily H. [Mrs. John D.] Hammond, "The Parsonage and Home Mission Reading Course," *Our Homes*, III (September, 1894), 1.

20. *Ibid.*, 2; "The Committee on Social Service," *Missionary Voice*, V (February, 1915), 92; *Twelfth Annual Report of the Woman's Parsonage and Home Mission Society*, 103. In 1902 Southern Methodist women began working with women from other denominations to select reading material. This interdenominational group not only recommended books but also wrote them. Also, the society frequently recommended books for young people. Mrs. R. W. [Tochie] MacDonell, "Home Mission Reading Course," *Our Homes*, XIX (November, 1910), 5.

21. *Sixth Annual Report of the Board of Church Extension*, 30; Lella A. Clark, "History of .

Lucinda Helm answered these critics directly. Home missions, she contended, did not weaken foreign missions; rather, they supported them. In the first issue of *Our Homes* she wrote that through the periodical she hoped to call attention to home missions, for home missions "do not hinder, but build a stronger foundation under, Foreign Missions by removing that rock of offense to heathen lands, a disbelieving, unjust nation back of the missionaries sent to them." Helm spoke for most home mission advocates in her day when she argued that if missionaries from America were to prove successful, they must be supported by a Christian America. The non-Christian elements of the country's population, swelling with increasing immigration, must also hear the gospel, albeit a gospel also mindful of their material needs. They must give up those habits and beliefs that threatened America's religion and its national way of life. It was an argument that was to carry the day.

A second obstacle to home mission work in the early years lay in the seeming indifference of most Southern Methodist women to the work that was being undertaken. Although early membership grew rapidly, totaling over 15,000 by 1898, the number was but a small percentage of a denomination estimated to have approximately 700,000 women members. Helm lamented that the work progressed more slowly than it should. A few years later, Tochie MacDonell, a Georgian whose energy and leadership were so vital to the expansion of city work, complained that the women's home mission efforts were "just touching the great fields that claim the hearts and hands of our people." Like Lucinda Helm, MacDonell was born into a prominent family, her father being superintendent of the Georgia School for the Blind. Not only did she receive economic security from her parents, but they transmitted to her also the importance of social service work. She graduated from Wesleyan Female College in Macon and soon afterward married a Methodist minister, traveling with him as a missionary to Mexico. Upon their return to the South, she became active in mission work. She shared with Lucinda Helm a sense of the urgent need for the work but was frustrated by the problems encountered. She was certain that the early efforts, though often encouraging, were falling short of their potential.[22]

A great problem in the early days was finding women able and willing to assume positions of leadership. Mrs. T. F. Marr, the first corresponding secretary of the society in the Western North Carolina Conference, complained of the difficulty of "finding capable women who would serve as District Secretaries," although the few committed workers who were found "did not grow weary or faint-hearted, but with a courage inspired by faith in Him . . . the cause of Christ was aided." In South Carolina, the start was even more discouraging. Twice the women began work there with conference officers and a small number of auxiliaries, only to see the conference and local groups disband each time. Finally, in 1898 a lasting statewide organization was established. Frequently, a single capable and committed woman could spark the work of a district or even a conference or state. Yet organizing such new and far-reaching work was difficult among women often "afraid to speak in public and too timid to stand and read the minutes of the meeting."[23]

Another frequent obstacle to the growth of home mission work was the local pastor. Speaking at the second convention of the Parsonage and Home Mission Society held in Nashville, Mrs. M. A. Matthews of the Saint Louis Conference Society asserted that "the apathy of presiding elders and pastors is the chief hindrance to the progress of our work." Apathy in some places turned to disdain. A pastor in Hannibal, Missouri, attributed the demise of the local auxiliary in his church to "overorganization of the Mother Church" and applauded the death. Many

22. Lucinda Helm, in *Our Homes*, I (January, 1892), 4; Maria L. Gibson, representing the Woman's Board of Foreign Missions, to the Central Committee of the Woman's Parsonage and Home Mission Society, reprinted in "Correspondence Between the Woman's Parsonage and Home Mission and Foreign Mission Societies," *Our Homes*, VII (November, 1898), 5; Mrs. R. W. [Tochie] MacDonell, "A Message from the Corresponding Secretary," *Our Homes*, X (November, 1901), 5.

23. Mrs. W. R. Harris, *Fifty Years of Missionary Achievement, 1890–1940: Historical Sketch of Woman's Missionary Society, Western North Carolina Conference* (N.p., 1940), 16–17; Walter J. Herbert, *Fifty Wonderful Years, 1878–1928: Story of Missionary Work by Methodist Women in South Carolina, Methodist Episcopal Church, South* (N.p., 1928), 62–65; Maria Layng Gibson, *Memories of Scarritt*, edited and completed by Sara Estelle Haskin (Nashville, 1928), 16.

pastors feared that the organization would replace the work women were already doing to support the local church, a position some women supported. In addition, they saw the local home mission societies as too independent. They perceived such organizations as groups that would take marching orders from their own leaders.[24]

The leaders of the society were sensitive to these complaints and tried to allay them. They understood the progress of their work to depend to a significant degree on the cooperation of pastors and thus went to considerable effort to win their favor. Frequently, *Our Homes* published letters from pastors who complimented the work of the society. Articles in *Our Homes* stressed that the women did not wish to challenge the authority of the pastor; rather, they looked to him for leadership and hoped to aid his work. A pastor opposed or ignored their assistance to his own detriment; whereas the wise pastor in utilizing the home mission society found "himself the leader of a trained force for carrying on all departments of his work wherein women may labor." The efforts of the women gradually bore fruit. In 1907 the Reverend C. W. Byrd, pastor of the West End Methodist Church in Nashville, acknowledged that in the early years of home mission work many ministers mistrusted the society. It was, he pointed out, new and untried. In the intervening years, however, it had proven its worth. Now he believed it "the most useful and helpful to the pastor of all the organizations of our Church save only the Sunday School."[25]

Certainly the opposition the women encountered in advocating home missions was to a significant degree rooted in the perceptions people held of woman's proper role in society. The accounts of the women's struggle to achieve an expanded role in their denomination point to the opposition they met in over a half century of work. In the beginning years these perceptions were a frequent hindrance. A historian of the auxiliary at

24. Matthews acknowledged that she was quoting Mrs. T. M. Finney, corresponding secretary of the Saint Louis Conference Society. Mrs. M. A. Matthews, "How to Enlist the Preachers," *Our Homes*, III (December, 1894), 6; Howell, *Women and the Kingdom*, 54.
25. "The Pastor and the Home Mission Society," *Our Homes*, XI (June, 1902), 1. See also "Our Convention in St. Louis," *Our Homes*, II (August, 1893), 7; "Woman's Parsonage and Home Mission Society," *Our Homes*, V (November, 1896), 6; C. W. Byrd, "A Pastor's Estimate of the Woman's Home Mission Society," *Our Homes*, XVI (October, 1907), 4.

the Mulberry Street Church in Macon reported that the women there resented the "patronizing spirit" of the men in the church. Some of the women were offended by terms like *the good women* or *the elect ladies*, which the men used to commend the women's work. The women believed that, by initially limiting their work and placing it under the Board of Church Extension, the men showed their lack of trust in the women's ability and sense of responsibility. When the Louisville Conference Woman's Foreign Missionary Society met for the second time in 1881, it was announced that the auxiliary at Leitchfield, Kentucky, was working under disadvantages and would have to be disbanded. Someone made a motion that prayers be offered for the removal of the difficulties. When another asked what the difficulties were, the reply was "Husbands." [26] This particular group was concerned with foreign missions, but the circumstances were frequently the same for women undertaking home missions.

Still, in the late nineteenth century, Southern Methodist women were discovering new opportunities for service in home missions, and church work was often a respectable outlet for women's energies. As Lucinda Helm reviewed the beginning years she could find satisfaction amid the difficulties. Bishop Hargrove, she noted, had "made the call, and women brave and true have responded with the loving zeal that only a woman's heart can know. Contending against obstacles unexpected, battling against indifferences where we ought to find ready responses, soothing the jealousy of mistaken zealots for other organizations, but ever guided and helped by God, we have gone forward slowly in regard to numbers, but we have accomplished a great work." [27]

Writing in *Our Homes* in May, 1894, Lucinda Helm expressed her conviction that the church must take responsibility for the fact that the masses had strayed. The church had, Helm noted, wrongly permitted

26. Clark, "History of Home Mission Society," 9; Mrs. E. F. Goodson, "A Connectional Asset," *World Outlook*, XXIII (February, 1933), 15. Goodson, tongue in cheek, suggested that the prayers must have worked: "A pastor some years later said that in a long ministry he had never served a church in which there were so many widows."

27. Anne F. Scott, "The 'New Woman' in the New South," *South Atlantic Quarterly*, LXI (1962), 476–77; *Seventh Annual Report of the Woman's Parsonage and Home Mission Society*, 25–26.

other organizations to take care of people's physical needs. The poor "have very naturally gained the impression that she is not concerned with what they consider real life, that her province is the spiritual and the future, which do not appeal strongly to men whose wants are mostly physical and altogether present." The irony of this was, she believed, that the efforts of secular organizations had their stimulus in Christianity. She pointed out that understanding "Christ's doctrine of the kingdom of God on earth . . . gives to these movements whatever vitality they possess, while it is the failure of the Church to apprehend the teaching of her Lord which gives to them their opportunity." In her report to the members in 1910, Tochie MacDonell, then general secretary of the Home Mission Society, reiterated Helm's concern about the church's neglect of social conditions and reminded the women of their obligation. The church had to be persuaded, she argued, that "a perfect religious hope must include not only eternal life for the individual, but the establishment of the kingdom of God for humanity. . . . Nothing short of the persistence, of the clear vision, of the willingness to be laughed at for attempting such work on the part of the women could have ever prepared the Church to do the work of social reconstruction, which is recognized as a part of her ministry today." [28]

Taking their cue from advocates of social Christianity such as Walter Rauschenbusch, the women stressed the importance of extending Christ's kingdom on earth. Rauschenbusch believed that the kingdom, which he perceived as earthly and yet divine, was at the center of Jesus' teaching. Commitment to it led the Christian to aid in transforming society in harmony with the will of God.

Rauschenbusch was concerned about formulating a theological basis for the social activity of the Christian. The women read and applauded Rauschenbusch's theory, but they focused on the practical extension of the kingdom. To extend Christ's kingdom on earth meant, at its core, alleviating physical want. This message the church had ignored to its own peril. "Genuine goodness," argued Sarah B. Cooper of San Francisco, "is something more than mere self-seeking for eternity. It is some-

28. Lucinda Helm, "The Church and Philanthropic Organizations," *Our Homes*, III (May, 1894), 8; *Twenty-fourth Annual Report of the Woman's Home Mission Society*, 43.

thing more than that sort of pious living which means little else than a safe and sagacious investment in the skies." Rather, she believed, it involved "working together with God in this world for the uplifting and advancement of the human race. It is a seeking to lessen the pains and burdens of life among the toilers and the strugglers." Mrs. James McCulloch reminded her readers that no woman should be so completely absorbed in personal matters "whether of salvation or anything else" that she had inadequate time to know about the social conditions of others.[29]

The women believed that this obviously meant special concern for those in greatest need. From her hospital bed in Hornell, New York, Lily Hammond wrote the Woman's Board of Home Missions that the message of Christ is that "our greatest debt is to the neediest." When she met him face-to-face, she hoped to be able to say that she had done her best "to help the folks that needed you most—the folks that were lowest down and farthest off—the folks who had fewest helpers and greatest need."[30]

What the message of Christ commended was a religion whose hallmark was service. The Bible lesson prepared for the local auxiliaries for May, 1917, reminded the women that the "fundamental aim in the life of Jesus was service." Three years earlier a member had argued in the *Missionary Voice* that the call to service was the "most distinct call that we hear from God. . . . A pure heart and a life filled with helpful deeds are the most perfect expression of worship." When Josiah Strong came to address the Home Missions Board in 1908, he reminded them that the "measure of our service to men is the exact measure of our consecration to God."[31]

29. Walter Rauschenbusch, *Christianity and the Social Crisis* (New York, 1907), xiii, 54, 65; Sarah B. Cooper, "The Kindergarten and Crime," *Our Homes*, X (October, 1901), 2; Mrs. James McCulloch, "Practical Studies in Successful Church Methods," *Our Homes*, XIII (September, 1904), 2. I have not attempted to argue that there was a widespread consensus among the women that the kingdom could be perfectly established on earth. On occasion, some women seemed to indicate that they thought this possible, but more often the issue was not directly addressed. What is clear, however, is their conviction that they should work to extend the kingdom.

30. Lily Hammond, "A Letter from Mrs. J. D. Hammond to the Woman's Board of Home Missions," *Our Homes*, XVI (July, 1907), 11.

31. *Missionary Voice*, VII (April, 1917), 123; Mrs. William A. Knabe, "The Call to Service," *Missionary Voice*, IV (April, 1914), 218; *Twenty-second Annual Report of the Woman's Home Mission Society*, 9.

Few passages of Scripture were as often quoted by the women as the account of the final judgment of the world in Matthew 25. For them, this passage indicated that a person was ultimately accountable to Christ for what he or she had done (or not done) for other human beings, particularly the poor and the disadvantaged. This, Lily Hammond believed, was a "better conception of Christianity" than the church had had throughout most of its history, "a conception based not on creed but on service." For too long the church had been overly attentive to doctrinal matters, and yet these discussions had done and would do nothing to resolve the world's problems. Christianity, the women contended, was "a life, not a creed. . . . One of the paradoxes of history [was] that it should have taken Christendom so long a time to give service an important place in Christian experience, inasmuch as the Founder of Christianity Himself made service the standard by which to determine real greatness." [32] It was one of the joys of living in the late nineteenth and early twentieth centuries that one could see the church (at least the Protestant Church in the United States) turning toward this "better conception."

Being an active part of the new emphasis on service was an even greater joy. Southern Methodist women saw their mission as "a great problem, a living, complex problem, not theoretic, not visionary, but intensely practical, to be so solved that the results will affect the lives, characters, and destinies of immortal souls." The words were those of Ruth Hargrove, whose husband, Bishop R. K. Hargrove, had initially aided in instigating the work by seeking help with parsonages. Ruth Hargrove would herself become a leader in the home mission work, succeeding Lucinda Helm as general secretary of the Home Missions Board. Over twenty years after Hargrove wrote, Mary Isabelle Downs, an officer of the Woman's Missionary Council, reiterated the same sentiment. For her, the task of home mission work was to "make the world the kingdom of our Lord and Christ." So grand a goal was achieved, she concluded, "not by wishing it but by working for it, praying with heart and also with

---

32. "The Bible and Poverty," *Missionary Voice*, VI (May, 1916), 237; "The Call of the South," *Our Homes*, XIX (September, 1910), 4; Lily H. Hammond, "Wasted Power," Nashville *Christian Advocate*, LXXV (August 7, 1914), 11; Henry Carre, "Bible Study for September: Jesus' Criterion of Greatness," *Missionary Voice*, XII (August, 1922), 254.

hand." They echoed Lily Hammond's sentiments that effective social action was "more religious by far than any amount of prayer for the salvation of the poor offered by folk who go home to idleness."[33]

From the beginning, the mission to extend God's kingdom on earth drew the women into intense activity to alleviate social problems. Yet, influenced by the writings of the leading spokesmen for social Christianity, the women began to give additional attention to the nature and form of the kingdom itself. In its 1911 report to the membership, the Institutional Church in Kansas City, Missouri, where the women were carrying on a variety of programs for the local community, expressed the growing emphasis on the communal nature of the kingdom. "The kingdom of God, the report noted, is a collective conception involving the whole social life of man. It is not a matter of saving human atoms, but the saving of [the] social organism. It is not a matter of getting individuals to heaven, but of transforming the life of earth into the harmony of heaven."[34]

In the early years, extending the kingdom had meant primarily charitable work among the needy, efforts often understood as groundwork for the religious conversion of those persons. In the first two decades of the twentieth century, there was new emphasis on the salvation of the world itself. Mabel Howell, who wrote frequently about the work and served as the first teacher of sociology at Scarritt College in Kansas City, Missouri, reminded the members in the Bible lesson for the local societies for June, 1920, that Christianity offers its own ideal social order. She concluded that "Jesus came to establish a new world order quite as much as a new individual." In Christianity alone is found "the ideal for which men are seeking and toward which they are . . . stretching forth their hands—a Kingdom of God on earth."[35]

33. *Twelfth Annual Report of the Woman's Parsonage and Home Mission Society*, 47; *Ninth Annual Report of the Woman's Missionary Council of the Methodist Episcopal Church, South* (Nashville, 1919), 84; Lily H. Hammond, *In Black and White: An Interpretation of Southern Life* (New York, 1914), 135.

34. *First Annual Report of the Woman's Missionary Council*, 416. The unity of society and social redemption were also key concepts for many leading Social Gospel figures (Hopkins, *Social Gospel*, 123–24).

35. Mabel Howell, "Bible Lesson for June: In Christ—the Ideal for the New World Order—the Kingdom of God," *Missionary Voice*, X (May, 1920), 158.

The saving work that Christ accomplished, the women believed, must be understood as more than the forgiveness of an individual's sin; rather, his atonement provided the foundation for the redemption of the social order. Personal salvation is only the beginning of Christ's work. "He does it so that we can help him get God's will done on earth as in heaven." With individual redemption came the call to service. Christ, Lily Hammond wrote, "expects us to invest our lives in making the world a safe and happy place, where righteousness is the basis of all human relations, where children may grow up to love and obey the law of justice, which is the law of brotherhood." [36]

The kingdom of God was not only "a world of regenerated people, but a world of people living in regenerated relationships to each other." Among its first laws were "Love one another, even as I have loved you," and "Do unto others as you would have them do unto you." The Woman's Home Mission Society, Tochie MacDonell believed, was an "expression of the Church of that faith in religion as a social force which makes possible the accomplishment of the ideal community where men are truly neighbors and love each other as themselves." For too long, Lily Hammond argued, the object of the church had been "to build up a kingdom in the 'other world,' remote, aloof, of the spirit purely." This world had been regarded as "necessarily evil, practically unredeemable." Such a view, however, these Southern Methodist women would not accept. This world was not evil; it was part of God's redemptive plan. And they had been called as his colaborers to realize its transformation. [37]

Nothing would be more misleading, however, than to conclude that these women were indifferent to the religious experience of the people whom they felt called to help. Their concern with the conversion of the individual may at times have waned, perhaps most noticeably during the

36. Lily H. Hammond, "Bible Lesson for January—the Task Christ Sets Himself and Us," *Missionary Voice*, XIII (December, 1923), 382. She reminds her readers that "if all who call his name were faithful to his ideal [of a redeemed world order] it could soon be achieved." Yet she cautions that we need concern ourselves only with our own faithfulness and "can leave the time of fulfillment with him."

37. "Thy Kingdom Come," *Missionary Voice*, V (January, 1915), 41; Mary Helm, "Thy Kingdom Come," *Our Homes*, XVIII (July, 1909), 1; *Twenty-second Annual Report of the Woman's Home Mission Society*, 41; Hammond, "Wasted Power," 10.

early twentieth century, but it was never extinguished. The first annual meeting of the recently organized Woman's Board of Home Missions in Dallas in April, 1898, passed a resolution calling "a great spiritual revival among our people" the "supreme need of the hour." Addressing the fourth annual meeting some three years later, Belle Bennett, then president of the society and for approximately thirty years one of its greatest proponents of social activism, cautioned the members that "the institutional work has been done unto the Lord, and not unto men, demonstrating to the world that the primary object of the organization is the salvation of souls; not simply the social betterment, nor the intellectual culture of the people among whom it works." In the early years, Tina Tucker wrote enthusiastically from Nashville of the revivals taking place: "O it was such a blessed privilege to have a part in it." Twenty years later she and her sister could be found seeking new converts among the unwed mothers at the Virginia Johnson Home in Dallas. The annual reports from the various schools and homes that carried on the mission work frequently included statistics on religious conversions as well as classes held or visits made. The workers at the Anne Browder Cunningham Mission Home and Training School in Dallas, for example, reported in 1899 that 85 percent of the over three hundred girls using the home since its opening "have been brought into a saving knowledge of the gospel of our Lord." Twenty years later the principal of the Sue Bennett Memorial School reported revival services on campus during which seventy-five were "definitely reached." Similar accounts were commonplace. Few of the women disagreed with the contention of Mrs. E. B. Chappell that "Protestant Christianity . . . requires an individual soul-commitment, which works spiritual changes within its followers." [38]

These southern women saw no irresoluble conflict between social activity and religious experience. Many were quick to criticize a religion that they believed unduly stressed the spiritual, but they did not deny

38. *Thirteenth Annual Report of the Woman's Home Mission Society*, 34, 105–106; *Sixteenth Annual Report of the Woman's Home Mission Society*, 63; Tina Tucker, "From Miss Tucker," *Our Homes*, III (June, 1894), 1; *Sixth Annual Report of the Woman's Missionary Council*, 146; *Ninth Annual Report of the Woman's Missionary Council*, 313; Mrs. E. B. Chappell, "Protestant Christianity Demands Soul Activity," *Missionary Voice*, XIII (April, 1923), 119.

that the spiritual, experiential element was a crucial aspect of Christianity. They sought to extend God's kingdom on this earth, but there is little evidence that they believed that this world was the limit of God's domain. Even those most sanguine about perfectly establishing the kingdom on earth seldom denied the Lord proprietary rights elsewhere. In any case, experienced faith in Christ was necessary for one to enter the earthly kingdom he initiated.

Tochie MacDonell argues that Belle Bennett easily mixed both elements during her long devotion to the home mission cause. Like mission activist Lucinda Helm, Bennett was a lifelong Kentucky resident. Helm had begun the work; Bennett brought to it new heights. She was the dominant figure during the first two decades of the twentieth century, serving as president of both the Home Mission Society (1896–1910) and the Missionary Council (1910–1922). From a prosperous family herself, she constantly fought against the forces of poverty and racial and sexual discrimination. Born in 1852, she experienced a religious conversion in her early twenties and subsequently made church work her life's work. She gained prominence among missionary workers for her fund-raising efforts to construct a training center for Southern Methodist women entering home and foreign missions. Achieving success against considerable odds, the school was opened in 1892 and named Scarritt after its largest benefactor. Thus began a period of uninterrupted service to the cause of home missions. "The motive of her . . . missionary zeal," MacDonell remembered, "was the building of God's victorious kingdom on earth. She sought to show the way of regeneration through Christ to the individual and fought to conquer the evil that clogs the salvation of society. 'Eternal life for the individual, the kingdom of God for humanity,' was the slogan of her life."[39]

Any seeming intellectual or historical inconsistencies in the coexistence of the two goals did not deter the women committed to mission work. They agreed with the claim of the *Missionary Voice* that there "*is no 'versus' between social service and evangelism*"; constant reiteration of the facts was necessary "to quell the unnatural conflict which so many people

39. Mrs. R. W. [Tochie] MacDonell, *Belle Harris Bennett: Her Life Work* (Nashville, 1928), 90.

insist on keeping up between two coordinate duties." Mrs. F. F. Stephens, who succeeded Belle Bennett as president of the Woman's Missionary Council, echoed these sentiments by applauding the widespread idea she found among the women in 1930 that "interprets the field of missionary endeavor as both individual and social, as both personal and institutional."[40]

A year after Stephens spoke, the Woman's Missionary Council established the Committee on Spiritual Life, primarily to initiate small prayer and devotional groups within the churches. Such efforts at enhancing spirituality had never been far from the attention of the women. Many of the local auxiliaries had been formed from groups that were originally devotional. Their meetings at all levels throughout the years were filled with daily devotionals and prayer hours. Such activities to promote spiritual growth enhanced rather than undermined attention to social needs. At a special spiritual life retreat of Southern Methodist women, meeting at Scarritt in September, 1931, the discussion of religious experience was mixed with a statement declaring its concern for "the grave conditions of the world about us" and its distaste for "the economic distress and human suffering that seem to be the result of selfishness in human relations." At a similar gathering three years later, Dr. Lavens Thomas of Emory told the women that, in a consideration of spiritual growth and Christian service, it was not "a case of *either—or*, but *both—and*. Indeed I might go further than that and say that life for one means life for both, while death for one means death for both."[41]

The distinction between the spiritual and social spheres, so precious to much of southern religion, including Methodism, and so embedded in its history, was antithetical to these southern women's ideas. They believed

40. "No Conflict Between Evangelism and Social Service," *Missionary Voice*, V (September, 1915), 388; *Twentieth Annual Report of the Woman's Missionary Council*, 53–54. Timothy L. Smith, in *Revivalism and Social Reform in Mid-Nineteenth-Century America* (New York, 1957), has persuasively pointed out the social activism of many evangelicals.

41. Sara Estelle Haskin, "Convictions Expressed at the Retreat," *Missionary Voice*, XXI (December, 1931), 39; Noreen Dunn, "The Spiritual Life School-Retreat," *World Outlook*, XXIV (November, 1934), 34. The attitude of Southern Methodist women apparently mirrors that of city mission workers in New York in the mid-nineteenth century. Carroll Smith Rosenberg, in *Religion and the Rise of the American City: The New York City Mission Movement, 1812–1870* (Ithaca, N.Y., 1871), 8, concludes that "these reformers desired both to save souls and control social stress—but saw the two goals as essentially the same."

that the work of women in other denominations had been seriously hampered by men who demanded a "strict separation of church and political activities," and they rejoiced that they, with more autonomy, had been able to bridge the separation. To Bertha Newell, longtime leader of the women's entire social service program, it was useless "to preserve old landmarks between some secular and sacred obligations."[42]

In her own life, Bertha Newell certainly preserved no such distinctions. Born in Wisconsin and educated at the University of Chicago, she married a minister of the Western North Carolina Conference. This transplanted northerner soon found herself at home in mission work. Her leadership of the social service programs covered almost two decades and involved her extensively in the mission causes of the 1920s and 1930s. Intelligent and energetic, she became one of the most active and outspoken workers.

Restricting religion to only spiritual matters made no sense to the women of Southern Methodism because they believed that Jesus' message and mission, in fact, defied such a division. His words and actions had certainly addressed physical as well as spiritual needs. The women believed that his death demonstrated that he cared about the whole person, not just a person's soul. It was "the *whole* man and *all* men for whom Christ offered up himself a living sacrifice."[43] As his followers, the women felt that they were called to minister to all of a person's needs and to seek to redeem his total life. To do so, of course, required seeking to redeem his environment.

---

42. Mrs. J. W. Mills, "Vice-President's Report," *Twenty-sixth Annual Report of the Woman's Missionary Council*, 54–55; Bertha Newell, "The Editorial Last Word," *Missionary Voice*, XVIII (February, 1928), 35. For a discussion of the emphasis that southern religion has placed on the conversion of the individual, see Samuel S. Hill, Jr., *Southern Churches in Crisis* (New York, 1967). Separation of the spiritual sphere of religion from the social is an idea that was widespread in all the South's major Protestant denominations from before the Civil War to well into the twentieth century. A historian of the MEC,S, has recently argued that through most of the 1920s the denomination was controlled by those who believed that the church should eschew practically all political involvement. After 1930, however, the progressives gained greater sway over church policy, and the denomination became increasingly involved in political matters. Robert Watson Sledge, *Hands on the Ark: The Struggle for Change in the Methodist Episcopal Church, South, 1914–1939* (Lake Junaluska, N.C., 1975), 205–212, 243. The women involved with home missions advocated this position long before the larger church adopted it.

43. "Forward," *Our Homes*, X (January, 1901), 1.

Some of the women saw the alleviation of a person's physical hard-ships as an important step in assisting his spiritual growth. Certainly not all the women gave voice to the conviction that material improvement was linked so closely to spiritual, but the idea was frequently expressed, particularly during the early years of organized women's work. Mrs. J. E. Chapman of the Holston (eastern Tennessee) Conference warned the delegates to the 1894 annual meeting that "the experience of all Chris-tian workers among the poorer classes [was] that, to reach the heart and save the soul, the wants and needs of the body must be attended to with kindness and promptness." MacDonell told the women that the develop-ment of the spirit was so dependent "upon the mental and physical con-dition that we scarce know where the one begins or how to separate it from the other." Similarly, Mrs. W. C. Ratcliffe of the Little Rock Con-ference urged the women at the 1896 annual meeting to support indus-trial education because "a great hindrance to the spread of the gospel *now* is to be found in the terrific battle that men are compelled to make for bread." There was, she believed, a great deal of truth in the claim that "neither a hungry man nor one cold is in a condition to accept the truths of the gospel." [44]

Years of experience would only confirm this for other women. In No-vember, 1929, Mary Downs, then secretary for home work among women, reiterated the conviction that social conditions influence one's spiritual life. Poor working and living conditions, she told her readers, "make it almost impossible for a person to be interested in spiritual things." Thus, she concluded, the purpose of the organization was "to lead in the establishment of better working conditions and relations and to see that opportunity is given for the acceptance of the evangelistic message of our Lord." She was reiterating the words of a fellow worker: "When the hungry are fed how easy it is then to talk to them about the Bread of Life, which completely satisfies." [45]

44. Mrs. J. E. Chapman, "Industrial Schools," *Our Homes*, IV (January, 1895), 7; *Twentieth Annual Report of the Woman's Home Mission Society*, 37; "Mrs. W. C. Ratcliffe's Address," *Our Homes*, VI (January, 1897), 9.
45. Mrs. J. W. [Mary] Downs, "The Evangelistic Message Through Personal Service," *Missionary Voice*, XIX (November, 1929), 30–31; Nelle Wynne, "Evangelism Through the Wesley House Community," *Missionary Voice*, XIII (October, 1923), 311.

It is not surprising, then, that when the society held training institutes in New Orleans to instruct some of the women in home mission work, a lecture by physicians on "physical laws, hygiene, how to tend the sick, what to do in case of emergencies, etc." would be followed by "a lesson on the spiritual visitation of the sick by pastors of the Methodist Church." The women never saw the two as very far apart. A northern friend told Mrs. Reid Wall, herself a Methodist worker, that she was impressed by the fact that southern women, though involved in mission work, "have not divorced your social service work from your spiritual life cultivation, but have developed them together, realizing that one is the outgrowth of the other, which is as it should be." A social program apart from the love and power of Christ would prove impotent; Christianity without social concern was, at best, a half gospel. Women of Southern Methodism believed that their work should be "social service saturated with the gospel of Jesus Christ, interpreted by hearts full of love of God."[46]

Amid the emphasis on extending Christ's kingdom on earth, while ever mindful of matters of the spirit, the women came to other conclusions about the world around them and its people. They never denied the necessity of God's grace in redeeming a person's physical, mental, and spiritual state, but they saw human beings as free, cooperative partners in redemption. "God," declared the women attending the spiritual life retreat at Scarritt in 1931, "has set limitations upon Himself. His plans for the salvation of men involve the cooperation of man."[47] The women, even leaders such as Lucinda Helm or Belle Bennett or writers such as Lily Hammond, were not given to the subtleties of involved theologies. They were practical women of action; theory alone had little attraction for them. Yet the religious ideas they held were integral to the work they undertook. People, they acknowledged, cannot be "lifted out of lives of sin and heathenism without the going forth of Divine energy on their behalf." God had a necessary role in bettering the social condi-

46. Reprinted from the New Orleans *Picayune*, in "From the Secular Press," *Our Homes*, IV (February, 1895), 1; Mrs. Reid Wall, "The Spiritual Life and Message," *World Outlook*, XXVI (November, 1936), 23; Belle H. Bennett, "Presidential Address," *Fourth Annual Report of the Woman's Missionary Council*, 76.
47. Haskin, "Convictions Expressed at the Retreat," 39. Hill writes that southern religious life "certainly deserves classification as 'Arminian,' because of its clear assumption

tion of this world as well. But the women emphasized not God's participation but the person's. The individual could freely respond, they were convinced, to God's call to assist him in the work of salvation. The women cared less about figuring out how God and human beings cooperated than about calling people to assume responsibilities. They disdained complacency; they celebrated human effort, most particularly in the growth of his kingdom on this earth. "We demand," Lily Hammond argued, "much more of God's grace than he ever promised it would do. . . . Almighty grace is a comforting doctrine when we are too ignorant or too lazy or too selfish to do our part of the job of saving the world."[48]

People were thus called to work for a better world. For not only were people free, they were also strongly influenced by their environment. Any possible tension between the two ideas did not bother the women. They believed that a person's life was influenced by his surroundings and that human beings must strive in their freedom to provide a better environment. "I do not doubt God's almightiness," Hammond wrote, "nor do I pretend to understand why, being almighty, He has chosen to so limit His own power that His own will cannot possibly get done in this world until men are willing to do it." She did not disagree, she contended, with the view that the soul is regenerated by the grace of God. However, she saw, as did some of her coworkers, a relationship between one's physical environment and one's spiritual condition. It was "our neglect of the living conditions of the poor" that had created barriers between them and God's grace, barriers "which can no more be removed by prayer alone, or by faith not 'made whole with deed,' than weeds could be removed from a corn field by the same process."[49] Grace, in other words, was resistible. The blessings of the Almighty had to contend not only with a person's recalcitrant will but also quite possibly with his degenerate surroundings.

Nurture, not nature, won the battle in the hearts and minds of these

---

that men are quite realistically responsible for, and capable of figuring in, their salvation" (*Southern Churches in Crisis*, 137). Although Hill understands *salvation* here to refer only to personal and spiritual salvation, the general thrust of the description would apply to the women active in home missions in Southern Methodism.

48. Mabel K. Howell, "Bible Lesson for May," *Missionary Voice*, X (April, 1920), 125; Hammond, "Wasted Power," 11.

49. Hammond, *In Black and White*, 134–35.

women of Southern Methodism. "More and more," *Our Homes* would tell its readers, "scientific investigation lays its stress not on heredity, but on environment; the differences between men are seen to be more the differences of opportunity than of inheritance." A person's behavior as well was attributable to his social situation. "Give our people proper living conditions," MacDonell argued, "and it becomes easier to live righteously." If the significance of the environment were stressed, the possibilities for change and hope were multiplied. It would be "through an ever-improving environment that the progress of the race will be chiefly promoted," Josiah Strong reminded the women, and since "we can practically set no limits to the possible improvement of environment, so we can practically set no limits to the possible progress of the race." [50]

Over the course of half a century, the opinions of the women on the perfectibility of their world varied. Yet essentially, they remained optimistic about its improvement. In the first decade of this century, Mary Helm, Lucinda's sister and a major figure in the home mission work in her own right as Lucinda's successor as editor of *Our Homes*, wrote that we not only "know as never before the condition and needs of the world, but we have the means as never before of doing the work of bettering and saving the world." [51] To provide evidence for her conviction, she centered the first two issues of *Our Homes* in 1908 on the theme of progress, "Progress of the Last Two Decades" and "Enlarged Opportunities."

More troubled times would bring more cautious analyses. But the underlying optimism about an improving world remained. The ravages of the Great Depression, Bertha Newell believed, proved the failure not of Christian ideals but of men to implement them. Mabel Howell insisted that the Christian would do well to "catch the inspiration . . . that comes from the optimism of Jesus. . . . He counted on our being able in

50. "The Immigrant," *Our Homes*, XIX (August, 1910), 2; Mrs. R. W. [Tochie] Mac-Donell, "Wesley Houses and the Social Work of the Woman's Home Mission Society," *Missionary Voice*, I (March, 1911), 48; Josiah Strong, *The Gospel of the Kingdom*, quoted in "Environment," *Our Homes*, XIX (March, 1910), 23. For a discussion of the importance of environmentalism to the nation's reform activities in the late nineteenth and early twentieth centuries, see Eric F. Goldman, *Rendezvous with Destiny* (New York, 1952), 85–131.

51. Mary Helm, "The Larger Opportunity of To-day," *Our Homes*, XVII (February, 1908), 3.

his strength to carry out the programme." The "programme" of course was his kingdom. Christ had initiated his kingdom on earth and, through his words and deeds, had provided a clear guide for its realization. The mission of his followers must be to work with him for its expansion. At the 1904 annual meeting of the Home Missions Board, Bishop E. R. Hendrix, the first president of the social-reform-minded Federal Council of Churches, preached the Sunday sermon "The Optimistic Christ; or the Undiscouraged Jesus." Calling the Sermon on the Mount the Magna Charta of the human race, Hendrix urged his listeners to work to spread Christ's earthly kingdom. Certainly the world had seen much evil, the women acknowledged, but progress, even if sometimes frustrated, was being made. The world was capable of improving; optimism was justified.[52]

It naturally followed that individuals were also capable of improvement. The Methodist tradition in America had long stressed that each person, though evil by nature, was through the grace of God capable of doing good. The women built on this tradition by emphasizing the importance of ethical activity and reinterpreted it, as did other Christians in their day, to point out the worth and potential of each individual. God, they believed, was "no respecter of persons. All have a share in his love; all may participate in his gracious favor; all are subject to the same principles of revelation." God, in other words, was a democrat, and each individual was of great value to him, with much potential for good. Christ helped bring persons to live better lives because of his trust in their inherent good. In his relations with others, he "proceeded from one fundamental principle—namely, that God sets an infinite value on each individual human soul." Similarly, none of us shows himself "so truly

52. *Twenty-third Annual Report of the Woman's Missionary Council*, 105; Mabel K. Howell, "The Appeal of Home Missions," *Our Homes*, XVII (July, 1908), 27; *Eighteenth Annual Report of the Woman's Home Mission Society*, 98. A different view of the attitude of the South in general is offered by C. Vann Woodward in his essay "The Search for Southern Identity" (in *The Burden of Southern History* [2nd ed.; Baton Rouge, 1968], 3–25). Woodward argues that southern distinctiveness rests on an experienced history that includes poverty, military defeat, and struggle with race relations in a nation that has a developed legend of wealth, success, and innocence. He notes that the racial experience in particular has made the South "basically pessimistic in its social outlook and its moral philosophy" even during periods of great national optimism.

made in the image of his Creator as when he passes on to other men this understanding of the worth and dignity and power of one personality."[53]

If each person were valuable to God, then surely each must be respected by His followers. If everyone, whatever his current situation, had worth, then it followed quite naturally that everyone's needs were rightfully the Christian's concern. For the women, social action flowed easily from a conviction of human worth. Through it, they not only helped others realize their potential, they also improved themselves. Belle Bennett reminded women that the Christian "cannot grow perfect except by helping his fellow-men." The "greatest good" achieved by the Woman's Home Mission Society was not the institutions it had started or the lives it had bettered but "the ever-growing goodness of the women who have lived and loved and wrought for them with God."[54] Home mission work brought improvement to the helper as well as the helped.

Thus there emerged among many of the women of Southern Methodism a passionate understanding of their Christian mission to their countrymen. It shaped their activities and not infrequently found itself shaped by them. This understanding centered on the conviction that the kingdom of God should grow on earth and that Christ, who initiated the kingdom, needed human help for its extension. Although this world was full of evil, the women saw it as basically good and capable of being redeemed. They saw persons in need of physical, mental, and spiritual help. They believed that the world in general and people in particular were capable of improvement. They held that environmental influences

53. The doctrine of Christian perfection or holy living was one of the most distinctive elements of the thought of John Wesley. Although denying the possibility of a static state of complete perfection in this life, Wesley saw the Christian life including growth in holiness. Albert C. Outler, *Theology in the Wesleyan Spirit* (Nashville, 1975), 65–88. For a more thorough discussion of this complex doctrine, see Albert C. Outler (ed.), *John Wesley: A Representative Collection of His Writings* (New York, 1964), 252–71, 283–98. Timothy L. Smith, "The Holiness Crusade," in Emory S. Bucke (ed.), *The History of American Methodism* (3 vols.; New York, 1964), II, 618, has suggested that the emphasis on human perfectibility by grace and the resulting "ethical earnestness" was the major Methodist contribution to the social reform movement of the late nineteenth and early twentieth centuries. Thomas Carter, "Bible Study for November," *Missionary Voice*, XI (October, 1921), 318; John S. Hoyland, *The Teachings of Jesus on Human Relations*, quoted in "The Missionary Society," *World Outlook*, XXV (July, 1935), 25; Margueritte Harmon Bro, "The Missionary Society," *World Outlook*, XXVI (March, 1936), 33.

54. *Nineteenth Annual Report of the Woman's Home Mission Society*, 24.

molded human lives significantly, and yet they argued that people are free to change environments. Although theirs was an understanding by the comfortable, it was especially concerned about the poor and neglected.

It was, however, a theory in particular need of a context. The way in which they understood their Christian mission made no sense unless Methodist women could exercise this mission in the world around them. The "world around them" was of course their native South, which was not always appreciative of the mission they felt compelled to undertake.

Chapter II / *Extending the Kingdom at Home and at Work*

Strong homes, the women believed, were the cornerstone of the kingdom of God. "The kingdom," Estelle Haskin wrote, "can never come except through the purification and the uplift of the center of our social organization, the home; and this is the chief business of the womanhood of our Church." A settlement worker, an officer of the Woman's Missionary Council, and a prolific writer for the women's mission work, Haskin made a major contribution to the work in the twentieth century. In her concern for the home, however, she was echoing the thoughts of the founder, Lucinda Helm. It was "the first mission" of every woman, Helm argued, "to win her home for Christ."[1]

Because of its vast influence, home was the beginning point of mission work. The women saw the home as "the basic institution of society and as a moral and religious factor which cannot be overestimated. It is the determining factor of all life." No other institution could substitute for it. One's environment played a significant role in influencing one's development, and no environment was as influential as the home. Upon the character of the home "depends the welfare of the whole social fabric." If one developed a nation of good homes, then would follow "a nation with high moral standards and a civilization ever tending toward the best spiritual as well as material things." Stress on the central importance of the family remained a consistent theme throughout the years. Lucinda Helm had pointed to its significance in the early years. As women were merging into the new Methodist Church many years later they were still being reminded that the family was the nation's oldest and most powerful unit—"the nucleus within which all life, both spiritual and temporal,

1. Sara Estelle Haskin, "City Mission Work Without a Trained Leader," *Our Homes*, XVIII (January, 1909), 9; Lucinda Helm, "My Home for Christ," *Our Homes*, IV (July, 1895), 1.

has its beginning and is nurtured during the critical stages of growth." Little wonder, then, that the women considered it "a subject of universal importance and one with which both church and state may well be concerned."[2]

But it was not only their own homes that concerned the women. They were equally disturbed by the conditions of the homes of the poor and the unchurched. They feared the consequences for those who endured these homes and for others as well. Lucinda Helm feared in particular the immorality that was, she felt, inevitable in a non-Christian home. "As mothers, wives, sisters," she wrote, "it behooves us to be up and awake to the importance of taking the Great Physician of souls into the homes of others, that the fearful contagion of sin may not extend to our own homes."[3]

This strengthening of home Helm believed to be a task unique to women. It was, in fact, a major motivating factor in the beginning of her periodical. Arabel Alexander, her biographer, reports that she once encouraged Helm to change the title of *Our Homes* to *Our Home Missions* or *Home Missions*. Helm resisted, explaining that she had been working for homes all along—at first, better homes for preachers and now, perhaps in the double sense of the word, better homes "for the homeless, friendless, Christless thousands everywhere." She wanted, she concluded, "even the title of my little messenger to bring that thought, the thought of *home*, to the front."[4]

The passing years would find the women expanding on Helm's thoughts. They would not forget the "fearful contagion of sin" and they would make more explicit its wide array of social wrongs. Some years after her sister's death, Mary Helm told the Home Missions Board at its annual meeting that the purpose of *Our Homes* was "to awaken and direct the interest and efforts of the women of our Church toward purifying and uplifting the homes and family life of the poor, the ignorant, the

2. Mrs. B. W. Lipscomb, "Spiritual Cultivation of the Jubilee: Our Homes," *Missionary Voice*, XVIII (April, 1928), 31; Tatum, *Crown of Service*, 59; "Home-making," *Our Homes*, XVI (July, 1907), 1; Mary Caldwell, "The Family in a World Crisis," *World Outlook*, XXX (April, 1940), 10.
3. Lucinda Helm, in *Our Homes*, I (May, 1892), 4.
4. Alexander, *Life and Work of Lucinda Helm*, 134.

unfortunate." The term *Our Homes* embraced all homes throughout the country. Yet the homes of the poor became a matter of special concern, for here, the women were convinced, was the source of many social problems. In mission work, Mabel Howell contended, Christian workers "need more and more to look to the home for the causes of poverty, intemperance, and crime." Lily Hammond noted, in describing the problems of southern factory workers, that it was not the homes of the well-to-do that determined "the stability of this country." Rather, she argued, it was the homes of factory workers and other "common people" that must be both "the nation's defense against outward enemies and its salvation from inward rottenness."[5]

The women's fundamental concern with the home was a reflection of their concern with the upbringing of children. Stable, moral, Christian homes were essential for a child's proper development. The home and the church, in close alliance, were "God's supreme agent(s)" in the proper rearing of a child. He must be provided the training, environment, and care "to enable him to attain the one hundred per cent standard of Christian life and service and to come into full citizenship in the affairs of God's kingdom."[6] A child improperly brought up could become forever immune to God's solicitations.

Therefore the women undertook extensive efforts on behalf of children. They started local groups for children of all ages, hoping to attract them whether or not their parents were churchgoers. They designated officers to direct the work, encouraged the children to collect funds for both home and foreign missions, and prepared special literature for their use. The women themselves undertook special studies on children. In 1912, over 100,000 pieces of material went to the local auxiliaries on child welfare, the study subject for the year. Three years later, the auxiliaries turned their attention to the adolescent boy and girl.[7]

5. *Twentieth Annual Report of the Woman's Home Mission Society*, 12; Mabel Howell, "The Deaconess and Home-making," *Our Homes*, XII (August, 1903), 3; Lily Hammond, "Some Southern Factory Problems," *Methodist Review*, LI (May–June, 1902), 351. The title of this periodical was changed to the *Methodist Quarterly Review* in 1903.

6. Mrs. W. A. Albright, "The Child—Its Value," *Missionary Voice*, V (March, 1915), 141.

7. *Third Annual Report of the Woman's Missionary Council*, 303; *Fourth Annual Report of the Woman's Missionary Council*, 161.

Such efforts, however, would never fully satisfy the women. They were convinced that "moral standards and religious faith are almost entirely the product of early training," and thus they could not ignore circumstances wherein these were absent. Kindergartens received widespread support from the women, and much of their city mission work included some kind of kindergarten program. "Hunt up the children of poverty, of crime, and of brutality," Sarah B. Cooper urged the readers of *Our Homes*, "just as soon as they can be reached." Schools were begun for poor children, immigrant children, and black children "with the direct purpose and aim of developing not only the mind but the character of [the] pupils, that they may become earnest Christian men and women, prepared to fill their places in the kingdom of God." Mrs. E. E. Wiley, founder of the Industrial Home and School at Greeneville, Tennessee, which took orphans up to age twelve, found it encouraging that many of the students were "trying to be earnest, honest Christians." This, she believed, was especially noteworthy, since some had come from environments that "would not be out of place in Dante's Inferno."[8]

The women supplemented their own educational efforts with widespread support for better public education. They were appalled at the South's public school system around the turn of the century, a system that was, in the analysis of one historian, "for the most part miserably supported, poorly attended, wretchedly taught, and wholly inadequate for the education of the people." They supported the increasing public expenditures, which in the South more than tripled between 1900 and 1913. At its annual meeting in 1906, the Home Missions Board resolved that "the time has come when our great Protestant Churches must take more active and intelligent interest in the matter of the public education of the children and young people of our country." Four years later, they reiterated their support of public education, specifically endorsing longer school terms, better school buildings and equipment, higher salaries for teachers, and compulsory attendance laws. The Woman's Missionary

8. Mrs. T. G. Ratcliffe, in *Second Annual Report of the Woman's Missionary Council*, 81–82; Sarah B. Cooper, "The Kindergarten and Crime," *Our Homes*, X (September, 1901), 1; Mary Helm, "Christian Education," *Our Homes*, XVIII (August–September, 1909), 2; *Eleventh Annual Report of the Woman's Parsonage and Home Mission Society*, 29.

Council continued this support, encouraging the establishment of a separate Department of Education within the federal government to discover better educational methods. In 1928 the council endorsed the Curtis-Reed bill, which provided for the department, and continued to support the idea in the years that followed. During the depression, Methodist women grew similarly concerned about "the complacency of this Republic over the rapid crumbling of the public and state schools."[9]

Support for public education was accompanied, however, by a desire that it include religious instruction. The interest in public education that the 1906 meeting encouraged in Protestant churches also included admonishment that "if they would be true to God and their avowed religious convictions," they should "inject into that school system by all lawful means religious teaching and Christian thought." The Bible, the women believed, had a rightful place in the public school classroom, and any attempt to exclude it would prove a "woeful mistake." They bemoaned its less frequent use and remained convinced that its "presence there violates no principle of our government."[10]

The women also carried on work at state colleges and universities. They established dormitories for Methodist women at a number of state campuses, the North Texas Conference completing the first in 1910 at the College of Industrial Arts in Denton, Texas. Later they sent workers to various campuses to plan and coordinate activities for Methodist students. In addition, they supplied teachers of religion to state schools as diverse as East Central State College in Ada, Oklahoma, and the College of William and Mary in Williamsburg, Virginia. Demand, however, outstripped supply because the women refused to send anyone who did not have an M.A. in Bible or religious education or a B.D. degree. Many schools apparently agreed with the women that the idea of the separation

9. Woodward, *Origins of the New South*, 398, 405–406; *Twentieth Annual Report of the Woman's Home Mission Society*, 28–29; *Twenty-fourth Annual Report of the Woman's Home Mission Society*, 169–70; Mrs. L. W. Hughes, "Council Indorses [sic] the Educational Bill," *Missionary Voice*, XVIII (July, 1928), 23; *Twenty-first Annual Report of the Woman's Missionary Council*, 153; Sara Estelle Haskin, "The Greatest Danger of the Depression," *World Outlook*, XXIII (July, 1933), 23.

10. *Twentieth Annual Report of the Woman's Home Mission Society*, 28–29; "The Bible in the Schools," *Missionary Voice*, XVI (July, 1926), 18; "The Bible in the Public School," *Missionary Voice*, XIV (June, 1924), 19.

of church and state must not be permitted to overshadow the need for religious training and had no quarrel with Belle Bennett's contention that "Church and State must work together for the highest good of the nation." [11]

In addition to their support of education, the women's concern with the development of children drew their attention to the issue of child labor. Increasing industrial development, particularly in the textile industry, had made child labor a common phenomenon in the South at the beginning of this century. In 1900, 30 percent of cotton mill workers were under sixteen, and over half of these were between ten and thirteen. Southern Methodist women were a significant part of a growing group of southerners concerned about these conditions. Reading and applauding the reform efforts of men like Edgar Gardner Murphy, an Episcopal clergyman, and Alexander J. McKelway, a Presbyterian minister, they pushed for more restrictive child labor laws. As early as 1901, *Our Homes* was demanding "the enaction of strong, imperative laws governing child and female labor both as to age and time." Children would not develop physically or mentally if "shut up in factories amid whirring machinery and unsanitary conditions . . . until mind, body, and soul are poisoned and dwarfed." The following year Lily Hammond reemphasized the point in her direct manner. "The most sinister thing in connection with our rapid growth as a manufacturing section," she told her readers, "is the increasing employment of women and children, and the utter lack, in nearly all the States, of any safeguarding of these workers by law." [12]

Effective laws were not easily realized in the South, however. Although by 1912 all southern states had adopted some form of age and hour limit, in the leading textile states the hour limit was sixty and the age limit twelve. In addition, the enforcement provisions of these laws

11. Tatum, *Crown of Service*, 236–38; *Eighteenth Annual Report of the Woman's Home Mission Society*, 104.

12. Woodward, *Origins of the New South*, 416. Murphy and McKelway were both leaders of the National Child Labor Committee, which was formed in 1904 to support state child labor laws. Herbert J. Doherty, Jr., "Voices of Protest from the New South, 1875–1910," *Mississippi Valley Historical Review*, XLII (1955), 58–62; "Forward," 1; Lily Hammond, "Book Review," *Our Homes*, XI (February, 1902), 3.

remained very weak. The limited success of these efforts stimulated the drive for federal legislation. In 1916, Congress passed and President Wilson signed the Keating-Owen Child Labor Act, thus excluding goods made by children under fourteen from interstate commerce.

The women had supported the law and applauded its approval. Many children were still being overworked and abused, Tochie MacDonell acknowledged, but she could still rejoice in the fact that because of the new law there would be "no cotton mill starvlings [sic] nor illiterates in the next generation." Her celebration was a bit premature. The Supreme Court declared the law unconstitutional. A second federal child labor law was also declared unconstitutional. Thwarted and disappointed, the women pledged to press harder for the enactment of state laws. In addition, they joined with others, despite "much opposition from husbands on the ground of State rights," in support of an amendment to the Constitution prohibiting child labor. Passed by Congress in 1924, it met particularly strong opposition in the South and was never ratified.[13]

The women's efforts on behalf of child labor laws were never completely successful. On an issue so important to industrial interests in the South, they inevitably encountered opposition. The women found themselves surrounded by husbands, relatives, and friends who opposed strict child labor legislation. That made grass-roots organizing for such legislation more difficult in the home mission societies, but the leaders' efforts did not abate. Belle Bennett, Tochie MacDonell, Lily Hammond, and Bertha Newell spoke early and emphatically about the working conditions of children; the denomination as a whole acted more slowly and haltingly. Their concern was primarily with children working in the textile factories, but subsequently they came also to include children laboring in agriculture and in street jobs such as selling newspapers and food. To them, the "God-ordained function of the child is not to produce, but to receive"—to receive a good education, proper recreation, and moral and religious training. A society that denied these benefits to its youth was in need of reform.[14]

The women's attention to education, child labor, recreation, health, and other social issues affecting children and the family did not prevent their active concern with more traditional moral issues. They strongly disapproved of what they perceived to be a society growing increasingly permissive in its behavior and moral standards. Several trends in the larger American culture received their critical attention. For the women, social progressivism found a happy marriage with strict personal conduct.

Because of their perceived negative influence on children, motion pictures were frequently the object of the women's concern. Belle Bennett acknowledged that the movie industry had much potential for good, but she was convinced that "the vicious forces of a depraved and unmoral human nature have seized it, and in a few years it has become, possibly, the most corrupting influence in our country." In her position as president of the council, she advocated increased government censorship, and her membership agreed. A decade later, Bertha Newell expressed similar sentiments in a letter to local auxiliary superintendents seeking their support for federal legislation establishing a Federal Motion Picture Commission to license only films without scenes of "exaggerated sex appeal," unnecessary and excessive violence, drunkenness, gambling, or "inciting dances."[15]

The women were convinced that movies had a significant effect on the children who saw them. Children who frequently attended movies were harmed "in attitudes towards teachers and friends, in deportment and scholarship, in co-operation . . . and self-control." The greater the number of movies children viewed over a long period of time, the worse the damage. The woman's section of the *Missionary Voice* printed the opinion of George D. Bivin, a physician "who has practiced for years in the

14. "The Question of Child Labor," reprinted from the Nashville *Christian Advocate,* in *Our Homes,* XI (December, 1902), 11; Gertrude Binder, "Child Labor, 1939 Style," *World Outlook,* XXIX (December, 1939), 14–15, 40.

15. *Eleventh Annual Report of the Woman's Missionary Council,* 39; *Fourth Annual Report of the Woman's Missionary Council,* 51; Bertha [Mrs. W. A.] Newell to Auxiliary Superintendents, July 15, 1930, in Commission on Interracial Cooperation Papers, Trevor Arnett Library, Atlanta University, Atlanta.

field of [the] nervous and insane." Addressing the National Picture Conference, Bivin claimed that movies contributed "to breaking up our homes and making our life impossible, so far as nervousness and complex conflicts are concerned." The effect on a child was especially harmful, for one could not "go before a motion picture and come away as he was when he went there." Movies made children in particular restless, insecure, and fearful. The women felt so strongly about this issue that they joined with the Catholic Legion of Decency in urging the boycott of "all motion pictures except those which do not offend decency and Christian morality."[16]

Movies were certainly not the only trend the women perceived as harmful to the development of children. Tobacco, "dirty" books, and suggestive dress all met with condemnation. As early as 1893, *Our Homes* was arguing that, given the claim of a well-known physician "that a tobacco user's chances of recovery from any malignant disease are lessened fifty per cent," it was time for "fathers and mothers [to] look into this matter, and see that their little boys do not take to the weed." In the 1920s, Bertha Newell urged the women "to examine the magazines for sale on news stands and at local drug stores, and to remove the filth that muddies the minds of our young people." She also encouraged parents to establish strict rules regarding their children's dress and behavior and to form mutual support groups in the face of increasing demands for relaxed standards.[17] Children being raised for the kingdom must be protected from the pitfalls of a too-permissive society.

Alcohol, the most pernicious element of the permissive society, was understood to affect the whole family structure, especially women and children, who were its unwitting victims. Southern Methodist women, at all levels of mission work, gave wholehearted support to the great Protestant crusade to eliminate its consumption. The women saw liquor

16. Martha Hazzard, "Do Movies Promote Lawlessness and Crime?," *World Outlook*, XXII (June, 1932), 22; "Again the Motion Picture," *Missionary Voice*, XVI (June, 1926), 26; Sara Estelle Haskin, "A Time to Follow the Catholics," *World Outlook*, XXIV (August, 1934), 23. For a fuller account of the tension between movies and conventional American values during this period, see Robert Sklar, *Movie-Made America: A Social History of American Movies* (New York, 1975).

17. "Effects of Tobacco," reprinted from the *Home Maker*, in *Our Homes*, II (no. 2, 1893), 1; *Seventeenth Annual Report of the Woman's Missionary Council*, 17; Bertha Newell, "Parental Problems," *Missionary Voice*, XII (August, 1922), 246.

as a great disrupter of home and society. "Drinking," historian Anne Scott points out, "was . . . troublesome to women for good reason. It led to a threatening social instability and created hardship in many families." The women opposed alcohol so strongly because they believed that it perpetuated sexual immorality, violent crime, and other social evils. Its effects on the home and on women were particularly detrimental. "Women," Mary Helm wrote, "have been the greatest sufferers from the liquor traffic; its curse has entered their homes, destroying their happiness; it has debauched and killed their loved ones, and the cry of thousands of broken hearts has been heard throughout the land." [18]

Confronted with such a problem, the women acted boldly. From the early years of the organized home mission effort, they condemned alcohol consumption and supported its restriction. They gave enthusiastic support to the Eighteenth Amendment and rejoiced in its passage. The Woman's Missionary Council even committed itself to work with other groups in bringing about worldwide prohibition. The women opposed any effort to weaken or circumvent the amendment and laws enforcing it. As a body, they did not openly endorse any candidate in the 1928 election, but the members of the council pledged themselves "to vote only for those candidates for offices, national, State, and local, who are committed by precept and example to maintain and uphold the Constitution of our country and to enforce its laws." The year following the election the council praised President Hoover for his support of temperance laws, and its members were warmly received by the First Lady at a White House reception. [19]

After the repeal of the Eighteenth Amendment, the women continued the crusade. Working primarily through their Committee on Citizenship and Law Observance, they pushed for the enactment and en-

18. Scott, *Southern Lady*, 147. I do not believe, however, that Paul Carter's contention that Prohibition became for many Protestants a "surrogate for the Social Gospel" aptly fits the women of Southern Methodism active in home missions. Although strong advocates of Prohibition, the women remained actively involved in attempting to correct other social wrongs (see his *Decline and Rise of the Social Gospel*, 31–45). Mary Helm, "Temperance," *Our Homes*, XVIII (February, 1909), 3.

19. *Fourth Annual Report of the Woman's Missionary Council*, 161; *Ninth Annual Report of the Woman's Missionary Council*, 181; *Twenty-second Annual Report of the Woman's Missionary Council*, 37–38; *Eighteenth Annual Report of the Woman's Missionary Council*, 162; *Nineteenth Annual Report of the Woman's Missionary Council*, 14–15.

forcement of state laws restricting liquor and for programs in the public schools to demonstrate the "deleterious effects of alcohol." They also attacked the role of the media. One reason for their mistrust of movies was the sympathetic light they believed motion pictures shed on alcohol consumption. "Alcoholic drinks," Martha Hazzard argued, without revealing her sources, "are drunk or displayed in about two-thirds of the pictures, and intoxication is shown, seldom in an unfavorable light, in about two-fifths of them." The Committee on Citizenship and Law Observance urged the women to exercise their influence "in every way possible to prevent the untruthful and pernicious advertising of liquor so insidiously used in publications, on the screen, and over the radio." In 1940 it commended the National Broadcasting Company for having imposed such a ban in its national programming.[20]

Divorce joined alcohol, in the women's view, as evidence of a permissive society and as a basic threat to the family structure. Despite their concern with the limitations placed on women, they saw divorce as no avenue to greater freedom. On this issue Bennett was unusually dogmatic. She argued "that no woman who is divorced from her husband, or who has been so unfortunate as to have had her name dragged in the mire of public scandal, should be elected to any office in a Conference or district, and certainly such a one ought not to occupy a place in this Board." The organization's Committee on Sociology and Philanthropy stood in basic agreement with her. To prevent easy divorces, it urged uniform divorce laws in all states. It recommended against placing in office anyone who had been made "a subject of public scandal" and opposed the remarriage of anyone divorced for "other than spiritual cause." The Woman's Board of Home Missions supported the action, and six years later (1914) the newly formed council similarly declared its support for "a strict interpretation of the disciplinary regulations against marrying divorced people."[21]

The women found it acceptable to regulate the creation of homes and

20. *Twenty-sixth Annual Report of the Woman's Missionary Council*, 148; Hazzard, "Do Movies Promote Lawlessness and Crime?," 48–49; *Twenty-ninth Annual Report of the Woman's Missionary Council*, 145; *Thirtieth Annual Report of the Woman's Missionary Council*, 158.

21. The women's attitude on divorce contrasted with that of many of the country's early feminists. Elizabeth Cady Stanton, for example, supported facilitating divorce procedures,

families as well as their termination. The same council that advocated "a strict interpretation" also supported moves "to prevent the marriage of mental and physical defectives." Lily Hammond concurred and argued further that no one "who is clearly a mental or moral degenerate should be allowed to bring children into the world."[22] The women's anxiety about home and family life led them often to accept considerable social planning.

The concern with home and family was never far from concern with the workplace. In the women's support of child labor laws the association is obvious. The intimate relation between employment and home was understood as valid for adults as well. Two special social service conferences, called in 1929 to commemorate the fiftieth anniversary of organized women's mission work in the Methodist Episcopal Church, South, passed identical resolutions emphasizing this point. "If our people of the industrial communities are to establish sound family life," the participants declared, "they must have a large measure of security of employment, wages adequate for family maintainance [sic] in health and decency, reasonable hours of toil, and working conditions that will permit all workers so far as in them lies to share in the abundant life."[23]

Although still heavily agricultural, the South of the early twentieth century experienced considerable industrial growth. The expansion so quickened during the 1920s that this fact has been described as the "overriding theme" of that decade for most southerners. It certainly became a focus of significant concern for these women dedicated to home missions. Southerners must not become "so drugged by the new wealth," Bertha Newell warned, "that we sleep when we should be asking ourselves whether the new industrial development is bringing costs and losses."[24]

---

arguing that unhappy marriages caused considerable suffering and immorality. Robert E. Riegel, *American Feminists* (Lawrence, Kans., 1963), 59; *Twenty-second Annual Report of the Woman's Home Mission Society*, 40, 162–63; *Fourth Annual Report of the Woman's Missionary Council*, 161.

22. *Fourth Annual Report of the Woman's Missionary Council*, 161; Lily Hammond, "Present-Day Philanthropy," *Methodist Quarterly Review*, LIII (January, 1904), 34.

23. Mrs. Wallace Rogers, "Jubilee Social Service Conferences," *Missionary Voice*, XIX (May, 1929), 24–25.

24. Tindall, *Emergence of the New South*, 71; *Eighteenth Annual Report of the Woman's Missionary Council*, 140.

Among the "costs and losses" of industrialization were inadequate wages and their subsequent effects on families. Tochie MacDonell complained that the "inability of men, eager and willing, to find work at a living wage is a disgrace to our civilization." Efforts to require employers to provide minimum, livable wages found support among the women. They perceived that the low wages paid men forced women and children into jobs, frequently in unsafe conditions and for long hours. When mothers were forced to work under these conditions, Newell argued, the health, nutrition, and even morals of their children suffered. She recommended day-care centers, supplemental incomes, and shorter working hours. When children were also forced to seek employment, problems were compounded. Owen R. Lovejoy, acting secretary of the National Child Labor Committee, writing in *Our Homes*, warned that when children are made to work because their parents are inadequately paid, "we reverse the evolutionary process in human development and condemn the family to inevitable disintegration." Such situations undermined the stability of the home.[25]

The women condemned inadequate wages generally, but they saw them as a particular problem for their own sex. They decried statistics that indicated to them "that in every line of industry and also in professional life men receive much larger wages or salary than women doing the same work." Part of the concern with this "double standard" was the obvious discrimination it demonstrated against women. But another part of the concern, expressed particularly often in the early years of this century, had to do with a woman's moral life. No single woman, Mrs. E. W. Cole argued in 1913, could live "comfortably and healthfully" on less than nine dollars a week, and yet, she claimed, the average woman's wage was only six. She suggested that a woman was paid such low wages, "since the path of shame is always open to her."[26]

25. Mrs. R. W. [Tochie] MacDonell, "The Church and Labor," *Missionary Voice*, V (April, 1915), 159–60; Bertha Newell, "Wage-Earning Mothers and Their Children," *Missionary Voice*, XIV (November, 1924), 23. Women formed an especially large part of the work force in the southern textile industry—approximately 40 percent in 1928, with about 30 percent of this total being both wives and mothers. Elmer T. Clark, *The Church and the World Parish* (Nashville, 1929), 294–302; Owen R. Lovejoy, "Effect of Child Labor on the Family," *Our Homes*, XVI (December, 1907), 7.

26. "What Is the Work of Our Women?," *Our Homes*, XVI (December, 1907), 1; Mrs.

The women responded to this problem in a variety of ways. In many cities they opened inexpensive boarding and rooming houses for single women, though they made clear that employers were not to use these as excuses for paying low wages. In addition, they did considerable "rescue work" among "fallen" women, often providing a home for a number of women within a city. The Woman's Missionary Council urged all city officials to take the necessary steps to abolish prostitution and suggested that "the names of owners of property used for immoral purposes be secured, that the force of public opinion may, if necessary, be brought to bear to prevent this sacrifice to greed." Yet for the women, many of these methods addressed the consequences of sexual immorality more than its causes. Thus they condemned its relation to the economic system and its roots in an immoral or impoverished home.[27]

In decrying the wages and working conditions of women, many perceived that women themselves contributed to the problems. Led by Mary Helm, many of the women expressed concern about working conditions for women employed as domestic servants. They were convinced of the hypocrisy of criticizing working conditions in industry without reforming their own domain, particularly in light of the large number of women (especially black women) so employed. The problems included long working hours, frequent isolation, poor food and lodging, and harsh employers. The problems were intensified because the absence of government regulation made each home a "law unto itself." The women encouraged greater standardization and regulation, but met with little political success.[28]

As was mentioned earlier, the South, despite growing industrialization and urbanization, remained a very agricultural and rural area throughout the half century of organized home mission work by women in the Methodist Episcopal Church, South. As late as 1926, approximately two-thirds of the denomination's members lived in rural areas and a large

E. W. Cole, "Woman's Place in Industry in Christian Lands," *Missionary Voice*, III (May, 1913), 284.

27. *Third Annual Report of the Woman's Missionary Council*, 405.

28. Mary Helm, "The Problem of Domestic Service," *Methodist Quarterly Review*, LXI (October, 1912), 705–718; Sara Estelle Haskin, "Voluntary Codes for Household Service," *World Outlook*, XXIV (August, 1934), 22.

percentage of its churches were located there. The Southern Methodist women most active in home mission work tended to belie these statistics. A large percentage of the conference and denominational leaders lived much of their lives in cities or towns, and much of the work was directed toward urban problems. City work was the focus of the social Christianity that so strongly influenced their efforts, and thus the women's attention was directed toward many of the same problems. Yet many leaders were familiar with rural areas, and even those in cities were influenced by the region's ruralism. The work there began more slowly, and although a number of mission concerns cut across urban-rural lines, the special problems of rural life received less attention for approximately three decades. During the 1920s, however, a number of workers were assigned to rural districts, and many auxiliaries readily began rural work. Often the focus centered on the lack of educational materials and inadequate health care. Urban auxiliaries frequently worked with rural ones, providing mission study books and other materials that might serve isolated areas as a portable library. Urban and rural women cooperated with existing agencies in securing county health units, promoting inoculations, treating hookworm and venereal disease, and providing clinics in public schools. In the 1930s, hundreds of local auxiliaries participated in the various projects undertaken, and the council maintained the Commission on Rural Development to oversee and promote these efforts.[29]

With these activities, the women attempted to address some problems of particular importance to rural families. They came to understand that the social conditions of rural areas, no less than those of cities, were inhibiting the development of stable homes. The Rural Development Commission argued strongly that rural communities desperately needed churches that were "spiritually efficient, with a program ministering to the needs, physical, mental, and spiritual, of every person in the community." Similarly, the council contended that rural congregations

29. Clark, Church and the World Parish, 282; Twenty-fifth Annual Report of the Woman's Missionary Council, 147; Thirteenth Annual Report of the Woman's Missionary Council, 162; Twenty-first Annual Report of the Woman's Missionary Council, 126–27. The commission, which was subsequently made a standing committee of the council, was part of the Bureau of Christian Social Relations.

needed "pastors who preach a social gospel as well as an individual gospel of repentance and salvation."[30]

Still these concerns for social betterment did not often lead the women to protest the system of tenant farming in southern agriculture. Widespread activities to meet special rural needs came rather late to the home mission work; concern over the plight of the tenant farmer came even later. By the late 1930s, some of the women were expressing sympathy over the harsh work, low wages, and poor living conditions that usually marked tenant life. But these efforts had little noticeable impact on a group that by then comprised almost a quarter of the region's population.[31] The women's program for the kingdom, shaped by their own backgrounds, was focused primarily on cities and towns.

In 1937, Bertha Newell, serving at the time as the head of the Bureau of Christian Social Relations, noted that the members had not been as active in economic reform as in other areas of social concern. She concluded that it was because appropriate action in the field was not self-evident. "The whole world of industry and economics has been in such chaos," she told the members, "that even the wisest thinkers and most experienced industrialists and authorities have differed and suffered perplexity."[32] Certainly the depression years were a time of economic confusion, but in these and other years, the women often seemed to take an uncertain approach to economic matters.

Clearly they were not comfortable with unrestrained capitalism. As Winifred Kirkland argued, the "Kingdom of God and the kingdom of greed cannot exist side by side." Excessive acquisitiveness violated the principles of the kingdom these women were attempting to extend. They believed that the conflict of America's "social order with the ideals of Christ is due to the fact that the organic principle of our economic system is selfishness, while the organic principle on which the kingdom is to

---

30. *Twenty-second Annual Report of the Woman's Missionary Council*, 145; *Nineteenth Annual Report of the Woman's Missionary Council*, 117.

31. *Twenty-ninth Annual Report of the Woman's Missionary Council*, 126; Ruby Van Hooser, "The Missionary Society: Working Together," *World Outlook*, XXIX (April, 1939), 31; Tindall, *Emergence of the New South*, 409.

32. *Twenty-seventh Annual Report of the Woman's Missionary Council*, 119.

be built is love." The *Missionary Voice* editorialized that the principles of competition and exploitation, which it perceived as fundamental to the American economic system, needed reexamination and labeled them "antisocial" and "unchristian." Jesus had advocated "brotherhood" and "cooperation." Therefore, what possibility was there "for the realization of that ideal under a system in which each is engaged in a competitive struggle for existence?"[33]

The women who led the home mission work and who wrote for the membership were distinctly uncomfortable with an economic system that seemed to reward raw greed. Generally economically well-off themselves, they were distanced from the world of business, and this helped give them a perspective at variance with most southern men's. Making money was a matter of less consequence. The women saw around them great disparities of wealth and they deplored such conditions. They were convinced that "abject poverty and great wealth are both a menace to individual welfare and social progress." They may have disagreed with Franklin Roosevelt's stand on liquor, but they applauded many of the recovery programs of the New Deal. Special protection for the working classes was, they felt, necessary. They believed that the "Christianization of economic life would guarantee to every man who will work a good livelihood and would enable him to make comfortable provision for old age."[34]

In light of this challenge to industrial capitalism, it is perhaps surprising to find that the women were seldom critical of the money-makers in their native South. In fact, their relationship with millowners, the entrepreneurial group with whom they worked most closely, would be better described as cooperative than combative. The women decried the working and living conditions of many factory employees, and yet their criticism of owners was remarkably restrained. When Lily Hammond bemoaned child labor conditions and the inadequate educational and rec-

33. Winifred Kirkland, "Jesus and Money," *World Outlook*, XXVI (February, 1936), 41; "Our Lord and the Golden Rule," *Missionary Voice*, VII (August, 1917), 252; "The Search for Social Justice," *Missionary Voice*, VII (November, 1917), 323.
34. Albert E. Barnett, "For the Devotional: The Material Side of Life," *Missionary Voice*, XX (August, 1930), 42–43; *Twenty-sixth Annual Report of the Woman's Missionary Council*, 151; *Twenty-fourth Annual Report of the Woman's Missionary Council*, 123.

reational opportunities available to children who worked in the mills, she refused to indict the employers. "For the present state of things," she argued, "the mill owners are not responsible." She maintained that "no one man can stem the tide of custom and hold his business together." Her prescription was more community support to provide needed services and stronger laws to regulate working conditions.[35]

Frequently the services the women provided in mill villages were supported by owners. Tochie MacDonell reported in 1908 that the Home Missions Board had had "repeated calls" from cotton mill owners seeking trained workers to assist in the villages; owners frequently bore the cost for most or all of the expenses of the mission work. Coal mine owners occasionally underwrote mission work among their employees. A barely fictionalized account of the work of one Methodist deaconess, Mae McKenzie, published in 1910, portrays her mission to an Arkansas lumber mill town where "unrest and lack of fellowship between employer and employee made the Company resort to the last means of overcoming the evil that pervaded their camp—that of employing a deaconess." Although the thinly disguised May Kenny focused her attention on remedies for drunkenness, illiteracy, and other common plights of workers in mill camps or towns, she worked cooperatively with millowners in constructing their village along model lines and alleviating hazards in the workplace. Similarly, *Our Homes* urged women to seek the aid of millowners who might be expected to assist in mission projects such as establishing kindergartens or building chapels. Praises were heaped on owners who had already done so.[36]

There is little evidence that such owner contributions silenced criticism by the home mission workers. In fact, they continued to support

35. Hammond, "Some Southern Factory Problems," 353.
36. *Twenty-third Annual Report of the Woman's Home Mission Society,* 59; *Eighteenth Annual Report of the Woman's Home Mission Society,* 41; Juanita Brown, "Come Go Up with Me," *World Outlook,* XXVIII (December, 1938), 14–15, 30, 41–42; Cora G. Williams, *The Morning-Glory: Life and Work of Miss Mae McKenzie, Deaconess* (Nashville, 1910); "The Duty of the Home Mission Society to Our Factory People," *Our Homes,* XIV (September, 1905), 1. Liston Pope, *Millhands and Preachers: A Study of Gastonia* (New Haven, 1942), found that owners contributed significantly to much of the church work done in the North Carolina mill villages. Pope concluded (pp. 149–50) that such actions permitted owners to have considerable authority in church matters.

legislation, such as child labor laws, that manufacturers opposed strongly. They could also be critical of employers who showed no consideration for the well-being of their workers. Yet in view of their attacks on unrestrained capitalism, one wonders why they were not more directly critical of owners. Their hesitation may have derived from the fact that many of the women shared the social and economic status of the owners. Their acquaintances and even families would thus have often been the targets of any personal criticism. Further explanation is suggested by their dedication to harmony in the workplace. They were profoundly bothered by the growing antagonism between employers and employees. Not only did this situation create economic disparity, it bred spiritual discord. It violated the kingdom's fundamental principle of love. The proper Christian attitude between labor and capital, settlement worker Mary DeBardeleben argued, was "co-operation between the two." [37]

The people who came to work in the southern textile industry in the early decades of this century were largely poor and unskilled. Coming from small farms and isolated mountain regions, they often found that the mill village offered some improvements in their way of life. Most of the owners were themselves native southerners, and many plants were locally owned. [38] In such a situation, the women were not inclined to view the owners as culprits. They perceived that the owners were themselves controlled in many ways by the circumstances of their environment. If an owner showed toward his employees special concern and kindness, even if wrapped in paternalism, then he deserved praise. He was an ally in the cause of economic harmony.

This did not mean that the women were content with the status quo. They believed that the economic system was unjust, but, unlike Marx, they did not think that conflict was necessary to correct it. Thus, they

37. Mary DeBardeleben, "May Program for Adults: Worship and Intercession," *World Outlook*, XXIII (April, 1933), 25. The women's reticence provides some support for the contention of Frederick A. Bode (*Protestantism and the New South: North Carolina Baptists and Methodists in Political Crisis, 1894–1903* [Charlottesville, Va., 1975], 1–7) that around the turn of the century, churches increasingly aligned themselves with the politically powerful advocates of "progressive" capitalism. His failure, however, to account adequately for the far-ranging social criticisms by groups such as these Southern Methodist women indicates the limitations of his thesis.
38. Tindall, *Emergence of the New South*, 76, 324–27.

said and wrote little about unions and offered no support for militancy. Progress was possible, but it was the sort of progress that comes through gradual reform, not dramatic upheaval. They would push hard for improved laws, and they would work to spread the message of mutual love. They believed strongly that the "interests of employer and employed are not antagonistic, but identical." It was a rather moderate attitude, though similar to that of no less a proponent of social Christianity than Washington Gladden, whose writings the women had studied.[39] In the context of the South, however, it often appeared radical. It led the women to see the world differently than did family and friends and it did not meet with wholehearted endorsement from the membership. The women who led the home mission work were convinced, nevertheless, it was the way along which the kingdom should be extended.

The women's attitudes and activities having to do with the home and the workplace were influenced by their developing thought regarding the nature of home missions. Increasingly they came to see that they should do more than aid the victims of social wrongs. Treating the effects of injustice was laying no solid foundation for the kingdom. To do that required closer attention to causes.

In 1904, Lily Hammond noted that "almsgiving which was its [philanthropy's] sum and substance in the beginning of the nineteenth century is but one of its minor elements in the opening years of the twentieth." People attempting to relieve social wrongs, she argued, were no longer satisfied to provide temporary relief; they wished to know why the condition existed and what could be done about it.[40]

The increasing emphasis on prevention and the concern for the child went hand in hand. When Sarah Cooper argued for kindergartens in 1901, she reminded her audience that "society's chief concern should be to remove the causes from which crime springs." She considered it "much more a duty to prevent crime than it is to punish crime." A child

39. O. E. Goddard and Mrs. R. W. [Tochie] MacDonell, *Making America Safe: A Study of the Home Missions of the Methodist Episcopal Church, South* (Nashville, n.d.), 60. Washington Gladden, *Applied Christianity* (Boston, 1899), 102–145, strongly encouraged business and labor to resolve their differences in a harmonious and mutually beneficial manner.

40. Hammond, "Present-Day Philanthropy," 26.

properly brought up would significantly lessen the possibility of crime, immorality, or poverty. Improving conditions in the family and the community would appreciably lower the number of maladjusted children. For the women, work with children, like other social work, "to be really effective must be primarily preventive." New understandings of social conditions, a writer quoted in the *Missionary Voice* suggested, demonstrated that it would have been wise for the Samaritan not only to save the traveler but to have the road from Jerusalem to Jericho patrolled to make it safe for travel and, in addition, to form something akin to a child welfare association so other children would not grow up to become thieves.[41]

The women were undergoing a significant transformation in their concept of home mission work. Their work had begun with the building and upkeep of parsonages. Soon it had spread to include charitable work among the sick and the poor. Yet even in the early years of the work, the significant concern with the home and the child had been directed toward preventing broken lives and social wrongs. In the early decades of this century, mission work itself focused increasingly on the sources of society's ills.

The women were convinced that "we must know causes before we can deal with conditions, for the source often explains results." In 1913 the Executive Committee of the council described an important function of social service as "the study and investigation of social questions such as sanitation, child labor, divorce, social purity, and temperance," thus distinguishing it from "local work," like parsonage upkeep and visitation of the sick. Therefore the women undertook to educate themselves and the world around them about social conditions. They read, wrote, and investigated their local communities. Bertha Newell rejoiced that women heading social service work in the local auxiliaries were "deserting the broad and easy way of visits, trays, and flowers for the narrow and difficult path of investigating 'sore spots.'" Thelma Stevens, a native of Mis-

---

41. Cooper, "The Kindergarten and Crime," 1; Kate B. Johnson, "Fundamental Problems of Child Welfare," *Missionary Voice*, XIV (August, 1924), 22; Emily Olmstead, "Young People's Bible Lesson—September," *Missionary Voice*, XV (August, 1925), 28. Olmstead is quoting an unnamed, imaginative source.

sissippi who had attended Scarritt and become the head worker at the Bethlehem Center in Augusta before succeeding Newell as superintendent of the Bureau of Christian Social Relations, praised the members for giving more attention to social issues such as education, health, and public safety in lieu of "the 'number of old magazines collected' or some similar welfare project that sometimes has very little of any permanent value."[42]

The women were optimistic that the patterns of the social world, like those of the physical world, were accessible to human knowledge. They rejoiced that the growing study of sociology and psychology was revealing more and more about social institutions and human behavior. Mabel Howell, who taught sociology at Scarritt and thus trained many women for mission work, stressed that social reform must utilize this additional knowledge. The "laws of philanthropy," she contended, "must be followed at least as accepted principles, obedience to which will secure the best results for the individual and for society." Social service work for the women was increasingly understood as a science. Constructive mission work was believed to include a knowledge of the conditions involved and an understanding of social laws. Social planning became an increasingly important part of home missions.[43]

The women could not be committed to social planning and eschew politics. They perceived the political process as integral to their vision of a better society. Tochie MacDonell wrote in 1911 that the Home Mission Society's members were "coming to realize that real betterment of the needy cannot be extended until laws are enacted and enforced which make some forms of poverty, suffering, and sin impossible." Years before they could vote, Bennett urged the women to seek laws to aid the causes they supported. A good, well-enforced law on behalf of the poor or helpless, she argued, would "do more to change and ameliorate their condition than all of the eleemosynary or philanthropic institutions that we

42. "Home Mission Literature," *Our Homes*, XV (September, 1906), 1; *Third Annual Report of the Woman's Missionary Council*, 242; *Twenty-second Annual Report of the Woman's Missionary Council*, 108; *Twenty-ninth Annual Report of the Woman's Missionary Council*, 125.

43. Mabel Howell, "Institutions for the Care of Dependents," *Missionary Voice*, VI (May, 1916), 210.

could establish in half a century." Although the women as an organization remained largely silent on the Nineteenth Amendment, most leaders—such as Belle Bennett, Tochie MacDonell, and Mabel Howell—favored women's suffrage and welcomed the new opportunities the ballot gave them to support certain political causes.[44]

More and more, the women saw politics as a necessary means to attain their desired social ends. "The state," Bertha Newell contended, "is God's ministry of organization, through which he must work." Failure in politics, she believed, was only an invitation to harder work. "When we work as hard as the devil works," she told the members, "we shall win territory from him that belongs to God. When we summon support for legislation in the interest of peace and education and good works of all kinds with the earnestness and power of the entire membership of our churches, we shall get that legislation." Similarly, Mary Downs reminded the women that they could not "follow Christ in the Church and turn . . . their backs on him in Congress. The vital Spiritual forces must be related to the civic life of the nation."[45]

Therefore, political activism was integral to the women's transformed understanding of their Christian mission. "Prevention," not "palliation," became their rallying cry, and prevention necessitated influencing the very structure of society. As a group that defined its mission as eliminating the causes of society's ills, they could hardly avoid political involvement. The women believed that most of these causes could be traced ultimately to a weakened family structure with its devastating conse-

44. *First Annual Report of the Woman's Missionary Council*, 126; *Twenty-second Annual Report of the Woman's Home Mission Society*, 39; Virginia A. Shadron, "Out of Our Homes: The Woman's Rights Movement in the Methodist Episcopal Church, South, 1890–1918" (M.A. thesis, Emory University, 1976), 96–98. The most obvious explanation for the home mission workers' reticence on women's suffrage is that during much of the same time period the most active members sought to gain "voting rights" for women as members of the church's deliberative bodies. One of the arguments used against the women in this struggle was that they were merely an extension of the suffragists. This charge they usually felt called on to deny, contending that representation and voting in church councils and the political ballot were different issues. By this separation they tried to avoid alienating men and women who opposed the Nineteenth Amendment.

45. *Fourteenth Annual Report of the Woman's Missionary Council*, 133; *Twenty-fifth Annual Report of the Woman's Missionary Council*, 102; *Twenty-fourth Annual Report of the Woman's Missionary Council*, 19.

quences for the development of children. They worked hard to establish sanitary, stable, moral homes. In addition, they did not hesitate to criticize the economic system, especially where it most threatened the family and proved most harmful to children. They wanted, in Lily Hammond's words, "God's free air in the homes of the poorest; a living wage for every worker; a chance to grow strong and pure for every child." Hammond admitted that this was "a far cry from present conditions," but she argued that "the vision has been given, the work has begun, the goal is seen as distinctly possible of attainment."[46]

The vision was the transformation of this world into God's kingdom. Increasingly, the women understood the extension of the earthly kingdom to transcend benevolent acts. The kingdom was not merely a place wherein people did good things; it was itself a good place, a place wherein the causes of evil were themselves expunged. This world, they believed, was capable of redemption. The women's developing ideas about the kingdom paralleled their growing understanding of true social service. The particular measures they supported were intended not only to correct social wrongs but also to spread Christ's earthly reign. His life and message had suggested and sanctioned them. They were an answer to both human need and divine command.

46. Lily Hammond, "The New Philanthropy," *Our Homes*, XIX (November, 1910), 2.

Chapter III / Extending the Kingdom to Immigrants and Seeking Peace

Immigrants came to America in increasingly large numbers after 1820—especially so in the final two decades of the nineteenth century and the first two of the twentieth. Although the percentage of foreign-born in the total population remained fairly constant during the period, the number of foreign-born in the United States in 1920 was more than double what it had been in 1880.[1]

To most native Americans, however, the number of the new immigrants was not as important as their origin. No longer were most immigrants from northern and western Europe. Increasingly they came from the countries of southern, central, and eastern Europe. In the final decade of the nineteenth century, over half of all immigrants to America came from these areas, and in the first decade of the twentieth, over 70 percent did. Though predominantly Catholic, those who came between 1890 and 1910 included many Jews. Often these immigrants knew little English, and their customs and habits were alien to native Americans. Significantly, they, much more than the immigrants who preceded them, crowded into the rapidly growing American cities, especially those of the East and the upper Middle West. They were an important part of the nation's transformation into a more urban and industrialized society.[2]

Only a small percentage of the massive number of new immigrants, however, found homes in the South. During the peak of immigration in the first decade of this century, little more than 2 percent of the South's population was foreign-born, compared with approximately one-fourth

---

1. John Higham, *Send These to Me: Jews and Other Immigrants in Urban America* (New York, 1975), 15. The portion of the total population that was foreign-born fluctuated between 13 and 15 percent during the period. The total number, however, advanced from under seven million in 1880 to over fourteen million in 1920.

2. John M. Blum *et al.*, *The National Experience* (2nd ed.; New York, 1968), 466–67. In 1890, 62 percent of foreign-born Americans lived in urban areas, compared with 26 percent of native Americans born of native parents (Higham, *Send These to Me*, 22).

of the population in New England and the Middle Atlantic states. Twenty years later, the figure for the South had dropped to less than 2 percent.[3] Save for a few locations, the immigrant was not a large element of the South's population during the late nineteenth and early twentieth centuries and, compared with immigrants in other areas of the country, did not substantially influence the region's way of life. Yet to the women of the Methodist Episcopal Church, South, interested in home missions, the immigrant assumed an enlarged significance.

Work among the immigrants was a part of the women's total city mission work. As has been indicated, the work that began in a number of southern cities during the 1890s continued to expand after the turn of the century. That work provided a variety of social, educational, and religious services to the needy in urban areas such as New Orleans, Nashville, and Atlanta. Special city missionaries were appointed by the women to undertake full-time work among the poor. Ruth Hargrove, the society's general secretary, reported in 1899 that seventeen workers were employed in ten cities. Under her successor, Tochie MacDonell, settlement houses were established with workers actually living in the community among those with whom they were working. The first settlement house was opened in Nashville in 1901; in the following year, houses were established in Atlanta, Dallas, and Saint Louis—the first of forty-five established during four decades.[4]

As the number of houses continued to grow, criticism of them from within the denomination did also. The major complaint was that the word *settlement*, associated with social service institutions begun in many northern and eastern cities, implied a secular effort, and one not wholly approved by some Southern Methodists. The leaders of the home mission work admired the efforts of these urban settlement workers, particularly Jane Addams and Graham Taylor in Chicago, but recognized that too close an association might create trouble. Moving quickly to extinguish the disfavor, Belle Bennett recommended to the Home Missions

3. Maurice R. Davie, *World Immigration: With Special Reference to the United States* (New York, 1936), 232.

4. Mary Noreen Dunn, *Women and Home Missions* (Nashville, 1936), 28; Haskin, *Women and Missions*, 202–204; Juanita Brown, "A Venture in Home Missions," *World Outlook*, XXX (August, 1940), 15–17.

Board in 1906 that the name be changed to Wesley House, and the board concurred.[5]

The scope of the work among immigrants and native poor whites in the early years outgrew the number of workers the women could supply. In addition, the leaders of the home mission movement grew concerned about improved training for the workers themselves. Some women were already receiving training, most in the Department of City Missions at Scarritt. The effort was expanded in 1901, when the Home Missions Board asked the managers of Scarritt for permission to place an instructor in home missions and sociology on the faculty. The request was granted, and Mabel Howell was selected for the position. In a further attempt to secure workers, the board established scholarships at Scarritt for women undertaking home mission training.[6]

Despite these efforts, the women could not secure enough trained workers to undertake the work they envisioned. Thus to augment both the quantity and the quality of workers, the board asked the General Conference, meeting in Dallas in May, 1902, to establish an order of deaconesses in the Methodist Episcopal Church, South. The arguments on both sides of the issue were aired in church meetings and periodicals. The women believed the order necessary to assure a sizable group of qualified and dedicated women to conduct home mission work. The church could maintain authority over their training and the location and quality of their work. Opponents countered that establishing the office of deaconess would weaken the motivation of other women to do home mission work. Such work, they contended, should be done by "all Christian women, and not . . . a selected few." The women who supported the deaconess movement heartily agreed. Led by Belle Bennett, they contended that deaconesses would not limit but expand the number of women doing the work. Trained workers could then more readily and ably train volunteers to assist them with the work.[7]

5. Dunn, *Women and Home Missions*, 30–32; *Twentieth Annual Report of the Woman's Home Mission Society*, 35–36; Howell, *Women and the Kingdom*, 188–89.

6. Dunn, *Women and Home Missions*, 39.

7. A. J. Lamar, "General Conference Proceedings," *Daily Christian Advocate*, XV (May 26, 1902), 4. A detailed discussion of the women's response to this and other objections is found in "Four Facts About Deaconess Work," *Our Homes*, XI (May, 1902), 1.

The major objection to deaconesses, however, centered on the question of woman's proper role in the church and in society. The structure of Southern Methodism permitted men alone, as conference delegates, to decide the deaconess question, and the men seemed divided on what social role women should play. Paul Whitehead, who argued in favor of the order at the General Conference, believed that the objections stemmed from "the Southern prejudice against woman being anything else but a member of the household and working in a social sphere according to her sweet will." In particular, many men felt that the proposal was only an unfortunate first step toward the ordination of women to the clergy. "I am opposed," J. B. McGehee told the General Conference, "to establishing a female hennery in the Church for hatching out female preachers."[8]

Barred because of their sex from entering the debate on the floor of the General Conference, the women had to respond to objections primarily through the press. In the pages of *Our Homes*, they asserted that the deaconess was not a preacher, nor was she to be ordained. She was not a "Protestant nun," nor was the home where she might live with a group of other deaconesses a nunnery. She was to be a trained worker and a consecrated Christian, serving under the authority of the church. During the meeting of the General Conference, Mrs. L. P. Smith, an active mission worker from Texas, was called to testify by a committee considering the proposal. Her acquaintance with deaconess work in England and her informed, forceful presentation were apparently significant in securing committee and General Conference approval.[9]

With the victory, however, the women were given more than they wanted. When the board had asked the conference to provide for deaconesses, it had also recommended that a joint committee of bishops and representatives of the mission boards, male as well as female, be set up to supervise the order. The General Conference chose, however, to give this responsibility to the Woman's Board of Home Missions. With cau-

8. Lamar, "General Conference Proceedings," 3–4. McGehee's language was ruled out of order by presiding bishop A. W. Wilson.

9. "What a Deaconess Is, and What She Is Not," *Our Homes*, XI (March, 1902), 1; Tatum, *Crown of Service*, 325.

tious enthusiasm, the women accepted, knowing that the eyes of the entire church were on them.[10]

At the annual meeting of the board in Atlanta in April, 1903, Bishop E. R. Hendrix consecrated the first five deaconesses of the Methodist Episcopal Church, South. Although over three hundred women would join the denomination's order and hundreds of others would work as trained city missionaries or home mission volunteers, the demand for workers frequently outdistanced supply, particularly in the early years of this century. The requests usually came from the local Methodist women themselves who were especially concerned about conditions in their own cities or areas.[11]

The individual histories of these efforts in towns and cities across the South record a variety of stories. In New Orleans, Lillie Meekin worked for over twenty years at the Mary Werlein Mission, providing food, clothing, and religious instruction to immigrants from a host of countries. In Biloxi, Mississippi, Minnie Boykin, arriving to find no building, no money for current expenses, and no local missionary society, secured a house and four volunteers and began work among seasonal laborers at the local fisheries.[12] Sometimes working alone, sometimes in cooperation with local pastors or men doing mission work for the denomination, the women carried on their mission activities. During the more than half century of the society's work, efforts were frequently undertaken on behalf of blacks and native poor whites, particularly those living in mill villages. However, immigrants were a major stimulus for much of the early work.

Southern Methodist women perceived the foreigners coming into this country as both a threat and an opportunity. The 1896 annual meeting of the society had warned of a "heathen and unpatriotic" foreign population moving into cities and towns. They came, the women believed, "with a spirit of infidelity and anarchism, endangering our institutions

10. "A Bit of Deaconess History," *Our Homes*, XVI (February, 1907), 1.
11. *Seventeenth Annual Report of the Woman's Home Mission Society*, 65; *Twenty-fourth Annual Report of the Woman's Missionary Council*, 97; Mrs. R. W. [Tochie] MacDonell, "An Open Letter," *Our Homes*, XII (August, 1903), 3.
12. Tatum, *Crown of Service*, 252–55.

and civilization." They had to be "Christianized" or they would "corrupt our people and destroy our own beloved institutions and substitute for our religion that of heathenism." Thus the women resolved to increase their work among them.[13]

The importance of the work was a frequent refrain in the late nineteenth and early twentieth centuries. "City missions is a most important department of our organization," Ruth Hargrove claimed, "and becomes a more urgent one as the low foreign element in large cities increases." There were "numberless" immigrant women and children, she argued, "for whom the services of women are imperatively demanded." Whatever the perceived need—religious instruction, education, medical care—the women attempted to fulfill it. "The heathen," Belle Bennett told the women, "are at our doors and in our homes." The American people had sought to profit from the immigrants and in exchange had given prostitution, drugs, and other "debauching evils of our own land." They needed the message and practice of the gospel. Similarly, Tochie MacDonell urged more women to commit themselves to mission work among immigrants and other poor. Too many, she believed, were hesitating because they were unconvinced of a clear call from God to undertake the work. They did so to the peril of themselves, their church, and their country. "If the Indians were approaching your house with hatchet and tomahawk," she asked the members, "would you wait for your father to order you to take up the rifle and protect your home?" She doubted that they would and told them that conditions in their day were every bit as urgent.[14]

Since the immigrant population of the South was relatively small, one might be surprised that this group commanded so much of the women's attention. Yet they perceived the foreigners as a real threat to both their religion and their country. Influenced by Protestant spokesmen such as Josiah Strong, who depicted the dangers of immigration, Catholicism, urbanization, and other "perils," the women had come to believe, in the

13. *Eleventh Annual Report of the Woman's Parsonage and Home Mission Society*, 43.
14. *Tenth Annual Report of the Woman's Parsonage and Home Mission Society*, 10–11; MacDonell, *Belle Bennett*, 104–105; Mrs. R. W. [Tochie] MacDonell, "A Word to the Young Women of the M. E. Church, South," *Our Homes*, XIV (September, 1905), 7.

early years of this century, that the major cities of the North were already
bearing the consequences of inadequate preparation. Large population
increases, primarily from immigration, were overtaxing resources. Ir-
religion, immorality, and poverty were already widespread.[15] The South,
and particularly its cities, stood as the next testing ground. That large
numbers of immigrants did not come to the South was perhaps not so
important in shaping the women's activities as the fact that the women
believed that they would come. They faced the possibility with mixed
feelings.

Many southern industrialists welcomed the trade and labor of immigrants. Not all the women, however, were happy about the prospect.
Mary Helm bemoaned the fact that the South wished to bring "into its
fair, inviting fields the worst elements of immigration—those of Southern Europe." The region was wrong in "seeking to infold this dangerous
foe in its bosom to poison its pure blood and to shatter its ideals." Lily
Hammond wrongly believed that the efforts of many southern businessmen to encourage more immigrants to come to the South would prove
successful. She was, however, more optimistic about the consequences
than was Mary Helm. Immigration, Helm warned, "is bound to come; it
is already coming, and bringing along with it immense possibilities both
for good and for evil." She was convinced that "if the South is simply to
hold its own morally and religiously for the next ten or twenty years, an
immense deal of home mission work must be done." Even the opening of
the Panama Canal brought new concerns about a flood tide of immigrants in Gulf Coast cities and new emphasis on home mission work.
"All the Protestant Churches in the country," Our Homes argued,
"should join hands and forces in making strongholds for Christ of these
strategic points, and do it before it is too late."[16]

Whatever their degree of optimism, in the years around the turn of the
century the women saw the situation as urgent. The battle that was

15. *Eighth Annual Report of the Woman's Parsonage and Home Mission Society*, 47.
16. Mary Helm, "From a Southern Point of View," *Our Homes*, XV (February, 1906), 5;
Lily Hammond, "Woman's Work for Women," *Our Homes*, IV (September, 1895), 6. For a
discussion of largely unsuccessful efforts to attract immigrants to the South, particularly
among businessmen, see Woodward, *Origins of the New South*, 297–99. "The Panama Canal and Our City Missions," *Our Homes*, XIII (March, 1904), 1.

being lost in the North must be won in the South. The fields of action were the cities. "No student of the situation [the increasing immigration]," the Reverend G. P. Mains told the women, "now fails to understand that the American city is the strategic and most critical battle-field for both Christianity and civilization." Dr. O. E. Brown, speaking at the 1910 annual meeting of the Home Missions Board, called Paul one of the greatest city missionaries, a man who "recognized that the city is the citadel of civilization, and . . . gave his life for winning the cities to Christ." Brown perceived the city as "simply the struggle between the organized forces of selfishness and the organized forces of service, and this last is none other than the Christian Church." [17]

Convinced of its importance, the women pressed their city work. They were concerned about all the poor, the uneducated, and the unchurched. Yet in the early years of the society, the immigrants created special concern. Not only were they poor, they knew nothing of Protestant Christianity or the nation's political institutions. Mabel Howell believed that the immigrant presented "*the greatest opportunity* the home Church has ever had," and yet she was convinced that all of them, unchurched and Roman Catholic alike, were in need of evangelical Protestantism with its "higher moral standards." [18]

The intensity and extent of religious bigotry varied among individuals, but certainly most of the women perceived the Roman Catholic faith of many immigrants as largely incompatible with strong personal morality and democratic ideals. Throughout the country, a writer warned in *Our Homes*, "this foreign element is coming to populate it, and bring with them the superstitions of the Roman Church." She was convinced that "the element is the lowest strata of their country, and they carry with them, wherever they go, the vileness of their depraved lives, to become a

17. Reprinted from the New York *Christian Advocate*, in "What Shall We Do with the Foreigners in Our Own Land?," *Our Homes*, VI (July, 1897), 3; *Twenty-fourth Annual Report of the Woman's Home Mission Society*, 17–18, 36. The women were certainly not completely sanguine about increasing urbanization. Commenting on Jesus' lament over the evils of Jerusalem, an unidentified writer noted that the cry had been "echoed by many followers of Christ as they looked upon our great and growing cities, helpless to stay the sin or relieve the misery that dwell therein" ("The Redemption of the City," *Our Homes*, XVI [August–September, 1907], 1).
18. Howell, "The Appeal of Home Missions," 26.

deadly contagion among our own people." Mrs. J. H. McCoy, head of the North Alabama Conference, also saw the immigrants as morally un-disciplined. She lamented that so many "come from priest-ridden coun-tries, where priestly absolution and the penance performed give license to offenses against God and man." Even Tochie MacDonell argued that immigrants who came from Latin America and southern Europe around the turn of the century had had their "sense of personal and political right . . . blunted by the domination of the Roman Catholic Church." She did not doubt the true faith of many Catholics but was convinced that it was not "a Church which can develop a people for republican government. Ignorance, superstition, and dependence mark those na-tions where it has held unquestioned dominion." Since she believed that more of these immigrants were coming to the South, she urged expanded home mission work.[19]

In the 1920s and 1930s the women would show more openness and tolerance toward Roman Catholicism and non-Christian religions. By this period, the vast influx of immigrants had been curtailed; like other Americans, the women no longer saw foreign populations as a threat to their religion or their political system. The First World War had shown them the possible consequences of intolerance and, along with their for-eign mission work, had given them more knowledge about the world. They could acknowledge the value of other systems. Since the early years of their own work they had encouraged cooperation among Protestant denominations. They would come to praise joint efforts by secular and church organizations to bring about social improvements. For more than two decades, they supported efforts to unite the various branches of Methodism.[20] But around the turn of the century, their fear of the conse-

19. Mrs. Marcus Wolff, "What Is the Object of the Parsonage and Home Mission So-ciety?," Our Homes, III (October, 1894), 8; Mrs. J. H. McCoy, "The Opportunity of a Wesley House in an Industrial Community," Our Homes, X (February, 1901), 56; Mrs. R. W. [Tochie] MacDonell, "The Need of Protestant Missions for Foreigners," Our Homes, XV (March, 1906), 5.

20. Evidence of this more catholic spirit can be seen in Bertha Conde, "Women Facing a New Task," Missionary Voice, XVII (February, 1927), 19; Sara Estelle Haskin, "What Is Our Missionary Urge?," Missionary Voice, XIX (October, 1929), 29; MacDonell, Belle Ben-nett, 217. For examples of specific ecumenical efforts, see Belle Bennett, in Twentieth An-nual Report of the Woman's Home Mission Society, 34; Mrs. J. W. Perry, in Twenty-fourth

quences of mass immigration frequently pushed them into condemna-
tions of Catholicism, less frequently of non-Christian groups, and most
stridently of those who pledged themselves to no religion.

Perceiving the immigrants as a threat to their church and their government, the women were determined to protect both. Their response to
immigration demonstrated how interrelated they perceived church and
state to be. "Give to the foreigner the precepts and gospels of Christianity," one member argued in *Our Homes*, "and you lay the basis for a life of
usefulness to the State and his fellow-men." The women saw no conflict
between their religious and political principles. "The government of the
United States," Mrs. J. W. Mills, a leader among Texas women, believed,
"was founded on the teachings of the Church." For her, good citizenship
was after all "only right relations of neighbor with neighbor, considering
the common interests of all, and the concrete value of persons as human
beings." These principles, she thought, mirrored "the simple teachings of
Jesus: Sacredness of human life, brotherhood, and the Golden Rule." [21]

The women believed that it was the Christian's duty to protect not
only the church but the state. Ruth Hargrove reminded them of Josiah
Strong's admonition that "the perpetuity of our republican form of government and Christian institutions depends upon the Church molding
the now alien population of our cities into harmony with the spirit of our
government." Home mission workers were agents of Christ, but they
were also protectors of the state. "The home mission problem . . . [was]
to Americanize and Christianize" immigrants, and frequently in that order. Patriotism became virtually indistinguishable from mission work. [22]

Work among immigrants, Southern Methodist women contended,
brought benefits to native Americans as well. It gave the people "protection . . . from vicious immigration"; yet it also aided "the rescue and

Annual Report of the Woman's Missionary Council, 43–44; Bertha Newell, "Social Service
Functioning in Woman's Missionary Council," *Missionary Voice*, XVII (June, 1927), 25;
Seventh Annual Report of the Woman's Missionary Council, 39.

21. Mrs. James Woods, "The Education of Foreigners," *Our Homes*, XII (March, 1903),
6; Mrs. J. W. Mills, "What Citizenship Tomorrow?," *World Outlook*, XXIV (January,
1934), 30.

22. *Twelfth Annual Report of the Woman's Parsonage and Home Mission Society*, 37; Goddard and MacDonell, *Making America Safe*, 12–13.

development of the immigrant by giving him our civilization and our religion." Some of the Methodist workers in the 1920s and 1930s may have more readily perceived the value of elements of other cultures and religions, but in the early years, workers believed unabashedly in the superiority of their own social and religious life. Just after MacDonell took over as the society's general secretary in 1901, she warned the members that since the United States "opens her doors to all mankind, it behooves her citizens to show, not by comparative study but by the Christ-filled life, the superiority of the Christian religion." [23]

The women had no intention of hiding their light under a bushel. Confident of their own cause and confronted with what they perceived to be the serious problems posed by immigration, they acted. They readily mixed social service with evangelical religion. Lillie Meekin, who worked with immigrants and other poor in New Orleans, noted that "most of these people are led to Christ by first relieving their needs of body, and there are many." Social help sometimes became an element of religious conversion. Although personal salvation was a more frequently stated goal of work among immigrants than it would subsequently become among other groups, it was coupled with concern about social conditions. In the same message in which she stressed the superiority of Christianity and encouraged immigrant work, MacDonell defined "the scope and aim of the Woman's Home Mission Society as serving humanity, building character, and saving souls." [24]

As with other home mission work, work among immigrants was to be directed toward the whole person. The growth of Wesley Houses also meant that many deaconesses and city missionaries lived in the foreigners' communities. These workers, thinking it important to understand the people they sought to help, were encouraged to learn other languages and customs. The women sacrificed time and convenience to make their work more effective, and they stressed that immigrants were

23. Mrs. John S. Stovall, "How to Increase the Membership and Effectiveness of the W.H.M.S.," *Our Homes*, XIV (August, 1905), 6; *Fifteenth Annual Report of the Woman's Home Mission Society*, 5.

24. *Twelfth Annual Report of the Woman's Parsonage and Home Mission Society*, 42; *Fifteenth Annual Report of the Woman's Home Mission Society*, 5.

victims as well as perpetuators of poor social conditions: there had been "slums in our great cities long before this modern influx of foreigners came." But underlying and motivating the work was their conviction that they must impress the ideals of a Protestant America on these new-comers to the land. Thus they shared their message of religious faith, good citizenship, concern and respect for the individual, and moral strictness. Effective home mission work among immigrants, the women believed, interpreted "the best in America to the foreigner."[25]

The women knew that America was not fulfilling the ideal vision in their own day. Yet they believed that it could and would prove a beacon to the world. The large number of arriving immigrants presented a great challenge. The threat they posed to religious, social, and political norms magnified the perceived need for home missions. Work among immigrants, Mary Helm wrote, was "the union of home and foreign missions." She called the influx of immigrants "a golden opportunity," a more optimistic assessment than she had made three years previously, because she now believed that those who were won to Christian service in America might well return to their native land for mission work.[26]

Yet the women believed that effective home mission work would have an even greater impact. If the world was to become Christian, America must lead the way. They agreed with Josiah Strong that the person who "does most to Christianize the world and to hasten the coming of the Kingdom [is he] who does most to make thoroughly Christian the United States." The women saw the world looking to America for leadership, not military but religious and moral. The example the world saw was badly sullied when a large foreign element of the population remained religiously destitute and socially disadvantaged. The work of foreign missionaries was severely hampered in the face of America's failure; mission work among immigrants in this country was a prerequisite to successful work around the world.[27]

25. "Preparation for Work Among Foreigners," *Our Homes*, XVII (March, 1908), 6–7; Goddard and MacDonell, *Making America Safe*, 90–92, 112.
26. Mary Helm, "What Does Our Name Mean?," *Our Homes*, XVIII (May, 1909), 17.
27. Strong quoted in Goddard and MacDonell, *Making America Safe*, 32; L. Helm, in *Our Homes*, I (January, 1892), 4.

Immigrant work, therefore, took on worldwide significance. For the women, the importance of the work could not be measured by a head count of foreigners in the South. They saw the immigrant, almost always non-Protestant and often non-Christian, poor, following customs and using a language at variance with those of Protestant America, as a threat to church, state, and even the kingdom of God itself. Those Southern Methodist women who pioneered home mission work were convinced that the kingdom of God they sought to extend must first take hold in America. The kingdom the women saw beginning here was decidedly homogeneous. They believed strongly in the virtue of the American melting pot, but the pot they envisioned had a distinctly Protestant flavor. The influence of a homogeneous Christian America, they were convinced, would then spread to a receptive world.

The vision was both grand and provincial, optimistic and yet overly suspicious. As the years passed, Southern Methodist women themselves, without expressly repudiating this view, came largely to ignore it in light of growing tolerance and ecumenicity. But it remains an important element in understanding the origin and development of their early work.

As the issue of immigration attracted the concern of Southern Methodist women engaged in home missions during the first few decades of organized work, so the issues of war and peace received considerable attention in the society's final three decades. The immigration restriction laws of the 1920s curtailed the number of foreigners coming to this country and reduced anxieties about their assimilation. But the international conflicts that dominated the first half of the twentieth century assured the foreigner of a continuing place in the national consciousness. As the years passed, the home mission work became increasingly diverse. Race relations, the role of women, industrial relations, and rural work all received the women's attention. Yet the issues of peace and international relations were also a significant focus of the work.

"The Woman's Missionary Council," historian Noreen Dunn Tatum writes, "was always a strong advocate of peace." Throughout its thirty-year history (1910–1940), the council pressed hard for the realization of peace and human brotherhood. During the quarter century prior to the organization of the council, there is scant evidence to indicate that the society concerned itself particularly with questions of war and peace. Emily Allen, acting editor of *Our Homes* after Lucinda Helm's death, supported the action of the United States in the Spanish-American War, although she prayed for the day when war would cease. Six years later, the membership was reminded by a writer in *Our Homes* that "if the lives sacrificed and the money spent in the Spanish war had been devoted to the redemption of New York and Chicago, the United States would have had more cause for rejoicing than it has now over its possessions of doubtful good in the isles of the sea." Working to improve the nation's social conditions, they were told, was frequently more beneficial to the country than military valor. The workers in the slums of the cities were themselves "true patriots," for poverty and immorality were as dangerous to the country and its religion as any military foe.[28] The issues of war and peace were not major national concerns in the early years of the work, and thus the women's attention was focused elsewhere. Yet they were not unaware of or unconcerned about the consequences of war; the years 1910–1920 would see them developing their views more completely.

Prior to America's intervention in the First World War, the women of Southern Methodism counseled the path of peace. At its annual meeting in 1915, the council protested "the cruel and useless waste of war" then taking place in Europe and pledged itself and the society's members it represented "to help in laying the foundation of a world-wide peace propaganda which shall inspire the coming generations with ideals which shall make war abhorrent and unthinkable." Belle Bennett told the assembled delegates that "prayer for world peace, a peace so grounded upon the great principles of the Prince of Peace that war and bloodshed shall be no more," was the world's supreme need.[29]

A year earlier, Bennett had interpreted the "overwhelming sentiment of this country against war, especially a war of aggression, and in favor of peace . . . as proof that Christianity has a conscience and that its con-

28. Tatum, *Crown of Service*, 362; Emily Allen, "The Spanish-American War," *Our Homes*, VII (June, 1898), 5; "Civic Versus Military Patriotism," *Our Homes*, XIII (October, 1904), 1.
29. *Fifth Annual Report of the Woman's Missionary Council*, 28, 62.

science is not dead." This sentiment, expressed in a statement Bennett had written with Bishop W. R. Lambuth and John R. Pepper for the denomination's Board of Missions, was widespread among men and women in Southern Methodism in 1914. Yet by early 1916, the women were less sanguine about the nation's direction. The *Missionary Voice* denounced steps to increase the size of the army and navy as "unnecessary, untimely, deceptive, reactionary, highly dangerous to ourselves, and a crime against war-cursed humanity." Increased military expenditures were seen as a retreat from "a Christian program of real peace." Reliance on military might was misplaced. The women saw "nothing noble or Christian in our talk of national defense." A greater need was preparation "to minister to the temporal and spiritual needs" of those who confronted the harsh consequences of war.[30]

When America did become involved militarily in the war, however, the council pledged its "deepest sympathy with our country in this time of national peril." Having opposed intervention prior to 1917, the women affirmed their national loyalty once the United States was involved in the fighting. Yet they remained deeply concerned about the war's consequences. In conjunction with declaring its support for the nation in 1917, the council called on the bishops to proclaim a day of prayer "that the barbarities of war may not take hold upon our nation." In particular, they hoped that "love and mercy" would govern the nation in its "thoughts and acts toward enemy peoples, but especially toward those in our midst from countries with which we are at war."[31]

30. Belle Bennett, W. R. Lambuth, and John R. Pepper, "An Address to the Church," *Missionary Voice*, IV (December, 1914), 644; "'Preparedness'—a National Peril," *Missionary Voice*, VI (January, 1916), 1; "Peace on Earth," *Missionary Voice*, V (December, 1915), 532; "The 'Preparedness' That We Need," reprinted from *Central Methodist*, in *Missionary Voice*, VI (January, 1916), 18.

31. *Eighth Annual Report of the Woman's Missionary Council*, 67; *Seventh Annual Report of the Woman's Missionary Council*, 40, 58. This attitude of restraint and concern stands in marked contrast to that presented by Ray H. Abrams, *Preachers Present Arms* (New York, 1933), who argues that most ministers and church members were zealous and nationalistic supporters of the American cause. Although many Southern Methodist women showed considerable fervor for the war effort, the expressions of concern indicate quite a number did not see it as an unmixed good. This position is closer to that of most theological liberals (see William Hutchison, *The Modernist Impulse in America* [Cambridge, Mass., 1976], 232–43).

The support many Southern Methodist women, particularly the society's leaders, gave the war was restrained by the realization that the conflict itself was evidence of human failure. The bloodshed and brutality of the war, Bennett argued, were forcing the Christian Church slowly to realize "that she has followed her Lord afar off." Jesus' message of international brotherhood and cooperation, Bennett believed, had fallen prey to "the proud and haughty spirit of nationalism, fostered and developed in Church and State, with patriotism as its slogan." Too many, she also thought, had come to the conflict "drugged with the wine of commercialism." Similarly, the *Missionary Voice* warned its readers not to claim "the flattering unction of superior virtue but with heart-searching and humble penitence seek in the school of sacrifice to learn the mind of God and make it [their] own." [32]

This attitude differs dramatically from the conclusion of one historian that Southern Methodists were "caught up in the general wartime hysteria and indulged themselves in orgies of printed hate." Many periodicals of the denomination depicted Germany and its people as corrupt, sinful, and atheistic. The war was a "righteous war," a "holy undertaking," and America assumed no taint by participating. [33]

The women of Southern Methodism could not help but be influenced by this nationalistic optimism, and some apparently shared in it enthusiastically. Yet more obvious is the failure to participate of women who headed the mission work and wrote for the periodicals. They recognized that no war was replete with unalloyed good and that the cause of the United States was not without some element of sin and guilt. They had advocated peace too strongly to fail now to see many of the unhappy consequences of conflict.

Any reservations about the fighting did not prevent the women from widespread involvement in activities on the home front. At the 1917 meeting of the council, the deaconesses and city missionaries offered their services to the government for special assignment to undertake

---

32. *Eighth Annual Report of the Woman's Missionary Council*, 67; *Seventh Annual Report of the Woman's Missionary Council*, 58; "As We Enter the War," *Missionary Voice*, VII (May, 1917), 130.
33. Sledge, *Hands on the Ark*, 50–51.

works of "mercy or social service." These and other offers were quickly taken up. In 1919 the council's Committee on War Work reported that almost two thousand Southern Methodist women had worked full time for the Red Cross, YMCA, or YWCA. Almost four hundred local churches and missionary societies had served as Red Cross centers. Wesley Houses and other council institutions served similar functions.[34]

In addition, the women were greatly concerned about the morality around military encampments in this country. Tochie MacDonell warned that too many teen-age girls in these areas were being diverted by "khaki and other military paraphernalia." An unidentified writer in the *Missionary Voice* urged that more older women be appointed to street patrols near the encampments, so they could counsel young women and supervise amusement places. She lamented that the "glamour" of the military uniform was "causing flutters of emotion in thousands of feminine hearts ordinarily calm and passive." She was convinced that some of the consequences of the situation were "so baneful that to counteract them has become one of the most pressing tasks thrust upon us by the war."[35]

World War I saw the women involved in a variety of tasks. Mabel Howell remarked that "the auxiliaries plunged at once into all kinds of war work. They decided for themselves that this was a concrete social service task." The women understood the war work they undertook as an extension of their mission work. Yet the leaders insisted that regular home mission work not be abandoned. MacDonell told members that "ours is the double task of caring for our young men in the camps and at the front and of maintaining our Christian institutions and activities unimpaired, that the soul of our nation may be nourished."[36]

In a nation caught up in the excesses of patriotism during war, the leaders' attitude of restraint was not always echoed by the membership.

34. Mrs. R. W. [Tochie] MacDonell, "Methodist Women and the War," *Missionary Voice*, VII (July, 1917), 200; *Ninth Annual Report of the Woman's Missionary Council*, 74, 235.

35. Mrs. R. W. [Tochie] MacDonell, "Committee of City Missions and Deaconess Work," *Missionary Voice*, VIII (August, 1918), 241; "The Girl and the Uniform," *Missionary Voice*, VIII (October, 1918), 307.

36. *Eighth Annual Report of the Woman's Missionary Council*, 141; MacDonell, "Methodist Women and the War," 200–201.

Settlement houses were sometimes the scene of community rallies to whip up support for the war effort, and at least one served as an army registration headquarters. No leader opposed these examples of national support but most cautioned against overzealousness. Some youth auxiliaries in particular, Mrs. J. W. Perry lamented, had become so engrossed in war work that they neglected the regular missionary activities.[37]

The women who directed the Home Mission Society did not glamorize the war. They perceived that war itself placed new strains on the nation's moral fiber. Families were separated, opportunities were created for personal immorality and economic greed, deep-seated passions of hate and racism were enflamed. Fearing moral consequences and concerned about the destruction that war inescapably caused, they longed for its conclusion. The fighting had temporarily shaken their optimism about their world. The kingdom seemed a more remote possibility than ever. But the end of the conflict permitted the women's underlying optimism to resurface more completely. Confronted with the horror of war, they searched for both meaning and hope.

A major sign of hope was the establishment of the League of Nations. Like most members of their denomination and most American Protestants, the women enthusiastically supported the effort at improved international relations; the council at its 1919 meeting endorsed the League. They regretted America's refusal to join and urged Congress to reconsider. Meanwhile, they praised the League's goals and supported other attempts at international cooperation.[38]

In the postwar period, the women's public statements show that they shared the widely held belief that from the hatreds of war would come a greater sense of human cooperation. The council's Committee on War Work argued in 1919 that the work the women had done during the fighting had brought them "into a broader human sympathy" with the world's people. The war itself had been "awful" but it had been waged for "justice and humanity, for the freedom of the nations, and for the doctrines of democracy and brotherhood." Even Belle Bennett, who had

37. *Ninth Annual Report of the Woman's Missionary Council*, 143.
38. Sledge, *Hands on the Ark*, 174; Miller, *American Protestantism and Social Issues*, 319–23; *Sixteenth Annual Report of the Woman's Missionary Council*, 160.

expressed often her anguish over the suffering caused by the war and who perceived more clearly than others its ambiguous consequences, seemed to share these sentiments. "Men and nations came nearer and nearer to each other through the heart anguish of those days," she told the women in 1919, "and the Spirit of God found in the waiting hosts a great training school where souls could be taught to look beyond race and color into other souls and know that to the remotest parts of the earth all mankind was one great brotherhood."[39]

Yet for the women of Southern Methodism, as for much of the country at large, the postwar optimism soon soured. They lamented the Senate's rejection of the Versailles Treaty and the League and were alarmed by the atmosphere of violence spreading across the country. Labor strife was accompanied by the fear and arrest of suspected radicals. In the South, as well as in the North, the revived Ku Klux Klan stirred the fires of race hatred, and riots and unrest burgeoned. Addressing the council in 1920, Bennett was more somber than she had been a year previously. She was anguished that "in our own favored land lynchings, riots, rapine, murder, lawlessness in all its forms stalk abroad. . . . We are yet groping through the aftermath of a struggle that drenched all Christendom in blood." Yet even here, Bennett was not completely disheartened. She believed that through all the turmoil the church was coming to a deepened conviction of the world's sin and its own participation in that sin. Nevertheless, the women were forced to conclude that they and others had probably placed too much confidence in the beneficial consequences of the war. In the days ahead, they would rededicate themselves more fervently to the cause of peace. "True, we made much of our patriotism [during World War I]," Mary Downs acknowledged in 1928, "guided by the high ideals of a democracy for the world." Still, beneath national loyalty, she believed that Southern Methodist women "ache[d] in . . . [their] hearts for those who were giving up their lives for this ideal." Now, she wondered, should they not "hold up the ideal of a world peace—a warless world?"[40]

The suffering of war and the disillusionment in its aftermath forced the women to reexamine their views on international relations. Before the

39. Ninth Annual Report of the Woman's Missionary Council, 235–36, 47.
40. Tenth Annual Report of the Woman's Missionary Council, 56; Eighteenth Annual Report of the Woman's Missionary Council, 88.

war, they had supported efforts to maintain peace and had thought war unnecessary and unlikely. Forced to accept the inevitability of the conflict, most were torn, as Downs indicated, between decrying its horror and hoping for its beneficial results. As the likelihood of these beneficial results lessened, they had to ask what had gone wrong. The problem, they concluded, was their failure, and the failure of others, to remain committed without wavering to world peace. The war had pointed out not the error of their idealism but the error of their judgment in thinking peace could be achieved through war.

Within a few years of the fighting, the women had firmly aligned themselves with the proponents of peace so widespread in American Protestantism in the 1920s. By 1921, Bertha Newell was decrying the fact that 88 percent of federal tax money went for military purposes and "a pitiful 12 per cent is the balance left for all other expenses of government." She demanded that current policy be reversed. Three years later, Mrs. F. F. Stephens declared in her presidential message at the annual meeting of the council that Southern Methodist women were joining others in "unrelenting opposition to the war spirit with its train of evils in the form of crushing taxation, preparedness, defensive measures, race and national prejudice."[41]

The council supported unsuccessful attempts to have the United States join the World Court, established to adjudicate international disputes. Members were urged to sign petitions favoring the Court, and these and personal letters of support were sent to members of the Senate. The women applauded America's signing of the Kellogg-Briand Pact, which renounced war and pledged its signatories to the peaceful resolution of conflicts. Bertha Newell, writing as superintendent of the council's Social Service Bureau, asked local societies to support the pact and encouraged them "to so study peace and the ways of peace that our beloved country and other countries may make these ways secure."[42]

41. For an account of the extent of this support for world peace, see Miller, *American Protestantism and Social Issues*, 317–32. Miller notes that the peace movement continued strongly into the early years of the next decade, but from the mid-1930s on, most major Protestant denominations were split over the subject of war and peace. Bertha Newell, "Women and Disarmament," *Missionary Voice*, XI (October, 1921), 306; *Fourteenth Annual Report of the Woman's Missionary Council*, 42.

42. Bertha Newell to Auxiliary Superintendents, January 24, 1931, in Commission on

There is considerable evidence that many of them did study peace. In 1929 the council established the Commission on Peace, which a year later became the Committee on International Relations and World Peace. Through the leadership of this group, the women began a more organized and concerted effort to create a climate of opinion to promote peace. They secured signatures not only from missionary women but from other church and community members pledging support for various peace issues and forwarded these to political figures. Throughout the 1930s, Southern Methodist women, urged on by their leaders, sent to representatives, senators, and presidents thousands of letters and petitions bearing tens of thousands of names, supporting efforts at world peace and advocating disarmament and reduced military activity. In their local auxiliaries they studied material such as Florence Boeckel's *Turn Toward Peace*, which contained chapters entitled "The Menace of Armaments" and "What You Can Do for Peace."

There is surprisingly little evidence that this championing of peace stirred conflict among the women in the interwar period. For the leadership, world peace became a major goal in the 1920s and 1930s. Among the wider membership, the goal also found considerable, even if less wholehearted, support. World peace and international cooperation became part of the vision that emphasized the dignity and worth of each person. In 1930 the commission declared that "the peace movement and the woman's movement are actually two phases of the same movement toward the freedom and recognition of the world of the individual." War and its attendant sufferings violated that view, and the women could not accept the idea that war might somehow enhance or inspire a higher quality of life. For the women, as they perceived the direction of history, peace was not only desirable but also practically "inevitable." The commission members maintained that "the question is not whether we shall have peace, but how soon we shall have peace."[43] Around 1930, the hope and expectation for world peace reached their highest point.

Interracial Cooperation Papers, Trevor Arnett Library, Atlanta University, Atlanta; *Twentieth Annual Report of the Woman's Missionary Council*, 135; *Nineteenth Annual Report of the Woman's Missionary Council*, 8; Tatum, *Crown of Service*, 363; *Twenty-second Annual Report of the Woman's Missionary Council*, 135–37.

43. *Twentieth Annual Report of the Woman's Missionary Council*, 189.

In the following decade, the women continued their quest, though its achievement appeared increasingly less certain. In 1933 the council wrote to President Roosevelt, urging him to declare an embargo on all arms and ammunition, to curtail naval building, and to seek an international agreement for the abolition of military and naval aviation. The council concurred with its Committee on International Relations and World Peace: they would "stand irrevocably for world-peace and for the abolition of war as a means of settling international differences." The following year the council denounced compulsory military training at state colleges and universities. In 1935 and 1936 the council passed measures protesting naval maneuvers in the Pacific, applauding Senate investigations into the munitions industry, and opposing appropriation bills for military expenditures.[44]

As the international situation worsened during the final years of the decade, the country, American Protestants, and the MEC,S, became increasingly divided over what response to make. Yet the women remained committed to a peaceful resolution of international disputes. They were horrified at the continuing growth of totalitarian regimes. Mrs. J. W. Perry, who succeeded Mrs. F. F. Stephens as the council's president, bemoaned the advance of "Communism, Facism, and Nationalism." She believed that these took "no account of man's spiritual needs, nor do they reckon with the utter futility of trying to build a permanent and harmonious world community with God left out." She acknowledged that she was terrified by "the progress these movements are making and the boldness of their claims."[45] The 1938 and 1939 council meetings also included denunciations of totalitarian regimes. Yet as much as the women disliked political developments in Germany, Italy, the Soviet Union, and Japan, they remained committed to a peaceful resolution of the world's problems.

Meeting in March, 1939, the council urged the United States govern-

44. The phrase is part of a declaration the committee had adopted from the denomination's Committee on Temperance and Social Service. *Twenty-third Annual Report of the Woman's Missionary Council*, 32, 135; *Twenty-fourth Annual Report of the Woman's Missionary Council*, 33; *Twenty-fifth Annual Report of the Woman's Missionary Council*, 21–22, 138; *Twenty-sixth Annual Report of the Woman's Missionary Council*, 28–29.

45. *Twenty-seventh Annual Report of the Woman's Missionary Council*, 47.

ment "at an early date to take the initiative in calling a world conference
for discussion of peaceful means for settling international difficulties."
Thelma Stevens, who had succeeded Bertha Newell as head of the Bureau of Christian Social Relations, expressed to the gathered women her
fear of the burgeoning nationalism in the country. A year later the council, in its final meeting prior to unification, was still not reconciled to the
inevitability of American involvement in the war. The Committee on
International Relations and World Peace recommended and the council
concurred that local auxiliaries sponsor peace programs in schools and
churches. War preparations were denounced, and members were encouraged to petition the president and Congress on behalf of peace.[46]

After unification, southern women joined with other Methodist women
in continuing to advocate the fading possibilities for peace. History was,
however, moving in another direction. When America entered the war,
the organized women did not criticize the country's involvement, though
they cautioned against excessive militarism. They carried out some support work for soldiers and war victims; yet they also turned their attention toward postwar planning, hoping to curtail possible discrimination
against minority groups and to establish international cooperation.[47]

The kingdom the women were extending was a kingdom of peace.
Discord and violence had no greater part in their understanding of international relations than in their views on the relations between capital
and labor. The support Southern Methodist women gave the nation's
wars makes it impossible to label them pacifists in any ideological sense,
but they were firmly committed to pursuing the path of peace even when
on occasion it appeared naïve to do so.

The peace efforts, as well as the women's response to immigration,
were an important part of the women's work. Both issues forced them to
respond to foreign populations. The immigrants were perceived as a
threat to cherished religious and political principles. A fundamental goal

46. *Twenty-ninth Annual Report of the Woman's Missionary Council*, 23, 125; *Thirtieth
Annual Report of the Woman's Missionary Council*, 165.
47. *Second Annual Report of the Woman's Division of Christian Service of the Board of
Missions and Church Extension of the Methodist Church* (New York, 1942), 178–79; Thelma
Stevens, *Legacy for the Future: The History of Christian Social Relations in the Woman's Divi-
sion of Christian Service, 1940–1968* (Cincinnati, 1978), 28–30.

of home mission work among them was bringing them into agreement with the women's own ideals and values. The work for peace came later and frequently reflects the development of the women's thinking. Their exposure to the horrors of war and their own foreign mission work gave them greater knowledge of and tolerance toward other cultures. Particularly in the interwar period, they were more critical of strident nationalism and its intimate relation to militarism, abandoning their own earlier rather chauvinistic expressions. International cooperation became the primary objective.

This shift in attitude paralleled developments among many of the nation's socially liberal Protestants. The atmosphere of nationalism that pervaded much of the early social concern among American Protestants was largely replaced by increased acceptance of cultural differences and a fascination with peace during the interwar period. The women of Southern Methodism were a part of these trends that affected groups across the nation. Yet another social issue was of special importance to their own region. Meaningful home missions in the South, the women came increasingly to recognize, had to include work among blacks.

Chapter IV / *Extending the Kingdom to Blacks*

The presence of a large number of blacks in the
South created a great challenge for the women of Southern Methodism.
We have seen that these women shared the social concerns of many
American Protestants and responded to these issues as they affected their
region. Yet no issue was as volatile in the South as that of race relations.
Although the work among blacks did not begin until around the turn of
the century and did not spread widely until the 1920s, it was a large part
of their home mission effort. Despite cultural pressures, they understood
their Christian mission to include outreach to a black population that
comprised approximately one-third of the region's people and was over-
whelmingly rural and poor.

As was true of many projects undertaken by Southern Methodist
women, the first initiative for work among blacks came from Belle Bennett. In her presidential address to the 1897 meeting of the society, she
reminded the women that the society had "done nothing for the negroes"
and that the denomination had "done but little." She was convinced
that "as an organization the path of duty is plain before us, and as the
Woman's Parsonage and Home Mission Society of the Methodist Episcopal Church, South, we must enterprise some special work for this great
race of people."[1]

In 1900 the Home Missions Board received a request from Paine College—a black school in Augusta, Georgia, begun as a joint venture between the MEC,S, and the Colored Methodist Episcopal Church—to
aid in constructing a building wherein black girls could be taught vocational skills. The board turned down the request because of inadequate
funds, but the following year Bennett reintroduced the matter. The
scene was again the society's annual meeting. At the conclusion of the

1. "Miss Bennett's Address," *Our Homes*, VI (January, 1897), 5.

Sunday sermon, delivered by Social Gospel advocate Shailer Mathews on the importance of Christian service, Bennett announced the formation of a project to raise $5,000 for the girls' vocational department at Paine. She gave $500, and, before the meeting ended, over $3,000 had been raised. The balance proved more difficult, however, and was not secured until the following year. Yet with this project, race relations work was begun, the first among organized white women in a southern church.[2]

The early years of this century saw the leaders focus increasingly on mission work among blacks. They encouraged black women to undertake their own home mission work, but largely they sought to determine what interracial work they should begin. "As a home evangelizing force," Tochie MacDonell declared, "we must define more clearly our relation to our colored sisters that live among us." She believed that "God has placed them in our midst, not from their or our volition, and we must help them to higher ideals of Christian integrity and to righteous living." The women understood themselves to have a particularly heavy responsibility to improve race relations. Lily Hammond reminded the board that it was "the Christian women of the white race who more than any other class can solve and dissolve the race problem, save our dear land from dishonor, and lift helplessness and ignorance into a new and hopeful life."[3]

The first woman to commit herself to full-time work among blacks was Mary DeBardeleben, the daughter of an Alabama Methodist minister. Educated at Columbia Teachers College and at Scarritt, DeBardeleben had intended to go into foreign mission work but was so alarmed by moral standards and living and working conditions among blacks on her family's plantation that she determined to undertake mission work among them. Discouraged by her parents and her bishop from undertaking such work, she received support mainly from her teachers at Scarritt.

2. Dunn, *Women and Home Missions*, 59–60; *Fifteenth Annual Report of the Woman's Home Mission Society*, 51–52; *Sixteenth Annual Report of the Woman's Home Mission Society*, 64; Lily Hammond, *Southern Women and Racial Adjustment* (Lynchburg, Va., 1917), 7–9.

3. *Fifteenth Annual Report of the Woman's Home Mission Society*, 9; *Twenty-first Annual Report of the Woman's Home Mission Society*, 18.

With this encouragement, she came before the newly organized council at its 1911 meeting to seek assistance. The council, hearing her controversial request in a meeting closed to the press and public, agreed to appoint her to work among blacks, and the South Georgia Conference pledged to pay her salary for the first year.[4]

She was sent to begin work in Augusta. Soon she opened a settlement house in an abandoned saloon that became the center of the work. Activities came to include recreation, cooking and manual skill or shop classes, a kindergarten, and religious services. Students and faculty at Paine assisted with the various projects, using the settlement as a sort of social work laboratory. Eventually, two additional buildings were used in the work and two satellite projects were begun for blacks in other areas of Augusta.[5]

Although the work grew, it apparently did not meet with unanimous community support. Mary Meriwether, who succeeded Mary DeBardeleben in 1913, reported "hearty co-operation" from local black leaders. Some years later, however, Thelma Stevens, who served as director of the Augusta work for over a decade, reported that, although some black ministers assisted the work, others appeared either disinterested or jealous. In addition, she noted that a few of the town's whites helped, but in general the "attitude of the majority of the white group is unsympathetic."[6]

Similar work soon followed in other cities. In Nashville, white women from the Methodist Training School and the society, responding to the appeals of a black woman, Sallie Hill Sawyer, began settlement work. The Bethlehem Center, as the council had named these projects for blacks, was run by a board of directors divided evenly between blacks and whites. One of the board members, Will Alexander, at that time a ministry student at Vanderbilt, was eventually to become a major figure in southern race relations work and a strong advocate of the work of Southern Methodist women. Students from Fisk, an all-black school in Nash-

4. *First Annual Report of the Woman's Missionary Council*, 21–22, 70, 77; Sara Estelle Haskin, "Women of the Left Wing," *World Outlook*, XXIII (February, 1933), 29; Mary DeBardeleben to Louise Young, August 31, 1936, in Hall, *Revolt Against Chivalry*, 71–72.
5. W. A. Bell, *Missions and Co-operation of the Methodist Episcopal Church, South with the Colored Methodist Episcopal Church: A Study* (N.p., 1932–33), 78–80.
6. Dunn, *Women and Home Missions*, 63; Bell, *Missions and Co-operation*, 81.

ville, and from Scarritt helped carry out many of the activities at the center. By 1940, eight of these centers had been established in various southern cities including Birmingham, Alabama; Chattanooga and Memphis, Tennessee; Spartanburg, South Carolina; and Winston-Salem, North Carolina. Funding for the work came from various sources including the council and local mission auxiliaries. The Methodist women would usually appoint one or two of their workers to direct the center with the guidance of an interracial board. There was frequently at least one full-time black worker as well. As was the case in Augusta and Nashville, black students and others in the black community often provided additional assistance.[7]

The society's first widespread race relations work to involve a larger percentage of the membership did not begin until after the First World War. The women were deeply bothered by the increased tension between the races that developed in the postwar period. Lynchings, race riots, and Klan activities led a number of southerners to seek methods to bring about better relations between the races. A variety of organizations—such as the Southern Sociological Congress, the Southern Publicity Committee, and the Commission on Interracial Cooperation—promoted improved relations. Some southern women, as well as men, were showing new interest in interracial work.[8]

At the annual meeting of the council in 1920, Bennett applauded these efforts. On the recommendation of its Committee on Home Educational Institutions and Social Service, the council also approved the establishment of the Commission on Race Relations "to study the whole question of race relationships, the needs of negro women and children,

7. Bell, *Missions and Co-operation*, 81–84; Dunn, *Women and Home Missions*, 66.
8. Southerners committed to social change in a variety of areas met annually from 1912 to 1920 in the Southern Sociological Congress, where they exchanged information and discussed a list of social problems. For accounts of some of these meetings, see James E. McCulloch's edited volumes of the proceedings: *The Call of the New South* (Nashville, 1912); *The South Mobilizing for Social Service* (Nashville, 1913); *Battling for Social Betterment* (Nashville, 1914); and *The New Chivalry—Health* (Nashville, 1915). The Southern Publicity Committee, directed by Lily Hammond, gathered and distributed news about black achievements. The Commission on Interracial Cooperation, a major force in encouraging a better racial climate in the South and with which the Methodist women worked closely, was organized in Atlanta in 1919.

and methods of cooperation by which better conditions may be brought about." The women, meeting in Kansas City, resolved "that as Christians and workers in God's Kingdom, we accept His challenge to show forth His power to settle racial differences."⁹ They were committing themselves to extending the kingdom to blacks.

Uncertain of how to proceed, the commission, chaired by Carrie Parks Johnson of Georgia, sought the advice of Will Alexander, head of the Commission on Interracial Cooperation, who had come to Kansas City to address the council about interracial work. He recommended that they accept an invitation to attend the meeting of the National Association of Colored Women's Clubs (NACWC) to be held in a few months in Tuskegee. Though the commission members had never heard of the association, they agreed to send Johnson and Estelle Haskin, who had strongly advocated creating the commission, to the meeting as representatives.

When Will Alexander informed Lugenia Burns Hope, a leading figure in the NACWC, of the creation of the commission by the Methodist women, she quickly issued them the invitation to Tuskegee. The wife of John Hope, the president of Morehouse College in Atlanta, Lugenia Hope represented a growing number of educated black women deeply concerned about the social condition of their race. In Atlanta she had created the Neighborhood Union, a settlement project that provided many services to the local black community. Hope saw the interest of the Methodist women as an opportunity to inform white women about problems faced and to enlist their aid. At the conclusion of the NACWC session, she arranged a meeting at the home of Margaret Murray Washington, wife of Booker T. Washington, between Johnson and Haskin and ten of the leading black women from across the South. The black women agreed, though some were understandably suspicious, imagining that the whites merely wished to discuss where they might secure better servants.¹⁰

Despite the unusual reality of an integrated meeting and the initial

9. *Tenth Annual Report of the Woman's Missionary Council*, 180; "Woman's Division, Commission on Interracial Cooperation" (Typescript in Jessie Daniel Ames Collection, Manuscript Department, Duke University, Durham, N.C.), 107.
10. Hall, *Revolt Against Chivalry*, 80, 87; "Woman's Division, CIC," 12–15. The author or authors of this document are not identified; Ames made marginal notes.

uncertainty and mistrust, the discussion that eventually transpired seemed to move the women of both races. Led by Hope, the black women spoke of their concern for their families and their race. Johnson, a deeply religious woman whose father and husband were both Methodist ministers, later reported that, after she heard the black women speak of their fears for their daughters and the safety of their families, "my heart broke and I have been trying to pass the story on to the women of my race." The black women appeared equally moved by the white women's concern. Charlotte Hawkins Brown, the outspoken president of the North Carolina Federation of Colored Women's Clubs and the founder of Palmer Memorial Institute in Sedalia, North Carolina, reported that the black women "were surprised to find the same things that interested us, the things we so desired, so much wanted, were the things the white women desired and wanted today." [11]

The impact of this initial meeting accelerated the race relations work of Southern Methodist women. With the encouragement of Alexander and the financial support of the Commission on Interracial Cooperation (CIC), which was at work establishing committees in hundreds of southern communities as well as southern states to resolve racial problems and tensions, Johnson began organizing a conference of white women leaders from various groups in the South to discuss race relations. The meeting convened in Memphis, October 6–7, 1920. Although a few invited women did not attend, approximately one hundred women were present, and about three-fourths of these were Methodists. Many, however, had only a vague idea of the meeting's purpose; a sizable number were members of the United Daughters of the Confederacy. [12]

11. From an address by Carrie Johnson, "The Business of Peace," National Convention of YWCA, Hot Springs, Ark., April 24, 1922, quoted in "Woman's Division, CIC," 15; from an address by Charlotte Brown, "Negro Women and Race Relations," meeting of Commission on Interracial Cooperation, YMCA Auditorium, Atlanta, October 7, 1921, quoted in "Woman's Division, CIC," 16.

12. Wilma Dykeman and James Stokely, *Seeds of Southern Change: The Life of Will Alexander* (Chicago, 1962), 88–96. Women of other denominations were also carrying out various race relations projects in the period before and especially after the Memphis conference. Southern Presbyterian women, under the leadership of Mrs. W. C. Winsborough, were particularly active. By 1924, organized women of eight religious bodies were affiliated with the CIC. See Ernest Trice Thompson, *Presbyterians in the South* (3 vols.; Richmond, 1973), III, 392; Robert B. Eleazer, "A Constructive Force in Race Relations," *Missionary Voice*, XIV (December, 1924), 25.

In addition to the white women present, four leading black women—Margaret Murray Washington, Jennie B. Moton, Charlotte Brown, and Elizabeth Ross Haynes—were invited to attend and speak. Alexander, one of four men present, recounted his uneasiness in the unprecedented situation of a formal integrated meeting, the prospect of which had also been met with uncertainty by both black and white participants. Carrie Johnson and Estelle Haskin opened the meeting by telling the assembled whites of their experience at Tuskegee, its impact on them, and the subsequent invitation to the four black women who would address the conference. The possibility was thus created for whites to leave at lunch. Although there is no indication that any did, tension and uncertainty over the gathering remained high. As the black women entered the meeting room in the afternoon, the white women rose. Spontaneously, Belle Bennett began singing "Blest Be the Tie That Binds," and the women, black and white, joined in with emotion and enthusiasm. Many of the women cried openly.

Each of the black women addressed the group. Margaret Washington spoke first. Born in Mississippi, she had graduated from Fisk and subsequently married Booker T. Washington, working with him at Tuskegee. A conservative in race relations, as was her husband, she assured her audience of her love for the South. Yet she deplored the "double standard" applied to black women and spoke movingly of the consequences of the inequities of black education. Jennie B. Moton, editor of the *Woman's National Magazine* and wife of Robert Moton, who succeeded Washington at Tuskegee, and Elizabeth Ross Haynes, a national officer of the YWCA and during World War I a worker with the Women's Bureau of the Department of Labor, spoke also of the indignities they and others had suffered because of racial discrimination and asked the assistance of the white women. Charlotte Hawkins Brown, who was born in New England but who had lived in the South for sixty years, closed the speeches with an emotional account of her forcible removal by a group of white men from a Pullman car on her way to Memphis. The irony, she reminded her audience, was that some of those white women present were on the same car.[13]

13. "Woman's Division, CIC," 20–69; Hall, *Revolt Against Chivalry*, 90–93, 286.

The experience of the Memphis meeting had a significant impact on many of the women present, one which they vowed to spread. The Federal Council of Churches called the conference "the strongest force yet organized in the nation in behalf of the colored race." Many blacks were inclined to agree. Charlotte Brown boasted that it was "the greatest step forward since emancipation." Almost twenty years later, in an address to the Federation of Colored Women's Clubs in Boston, Jessie Daniel Ames, herself a white southerner active in interracial work, reflected that the Memphis meeting showed that "the common ground upon which these two groups of women could meet and plan for the common good was that of religion. Other ways were tried but all failed." Her contention that churchwomen were the backbone of the movement for improved race relations was shared by Will Alexander, who later recalled that, after the Memphis meeting, "the most effective force in changing southern racial patterns has been the white women." Most of the leadership, he reported, had come from church organizations.[14]

Southern Methodist women were at the forefront of this movement. A Continuation Committee was appointed by the Memphis conference to pursue further interracial work, with Carrie Johnson as head. The committee, which was composed of representatives from each organization attending the Memphis meeting, subsequently became a part of the Commission on Interracial Cooperation. Previously, the CIC had been hesitant about including women in its work, but after Memphis this resistance crumbled. Carrie Johnson was selected to direct the new Woman's Division.

Buoyed by the spirit of Memphis, the Methodist women's council concurred with the Continuation Committee's recommendation that it and other women's groups undertake more extensive race relations work. The council encouraged local auxiliaries to form their own committees on interracial work. The women on these committees were urged to get to know leaders among the black women in their communities; to study housing, sanitation, and other social conditions in the black commu-

14. Quoted in "Woman's Division, CIC," 70, 82; Dykeman and Stokely, *Seeds of Southern Change*, 95; Jessie Daniel Ames, "Address to Federation of Colored Women's Clubs, 1939" (Typescript in Commission on Interracial Cooperation Papers, Trevor Arnett Library, Atlanta University, Atlanta).

nities; and to acquaint themselves with black achievements in art, literature, science, and other fields.[15] This was the start of an effort to establish
widespread race relations work among the women of Southern Methodism.

The leaders of the council were optimistic about the work they had
begun. Memphis had been a conversion experience for many of the
women. They had learned of the problems that blacks had to deal with
and something of the whites' role in those problems; they had seen the
concern of many black women for members of their own race. Johnson
admitted that she was "humiliated" by her ignorance and that of other
white women, but she was convinced that "these Negro women helped
us to see some things in a different light." The women were confident
that the relations between blacks and whites and the social and moral
conditions of blacks could be bettered. They were encouraged that some
black women desired improvement, yet they also sensed a heavy responsibility. Carrie Johnson spoke for most of the women leaders when she
expressed a belief that Christian women in the South had a unique opportunity. God, she contended, had for generations provided them "a
background of training and understanding for this world task [bettering
race relations] which has not been possible to any other women." They
were, she was convinced, "not unmindful of the increased responsibility
which rests upon us because of these facts" and they must assume "the
leadership in demonstrating the adequacy of the principles of Christ in
this unconquered field."[16]

The women in the local auxiliaries were not, however, quite as quick
to assume the mantle of responsibility. Bertha Newell recalled that "this
filtering down of inspiration and activity to the local auxiliaries was slow,
and at first rather discouraging—a fact which was due, however, more to
indifference than to prejudice." The council's Commission on Race Relations reported in 1924 that its work was slowed by a variety of difficulties
from inside and outside the organization, difficulties including condescension toward blacks and fear of social criticism. Nevertheless, by the
end of the first year of local work in 1922, over one hundred auxiliaries

15. *Eleventh Annual Report of the Woman's Missionary Council*, 194; "Woman's Division,
CIC," 19–21, 43.
16. "Woman's Division, CIC," 70–71; *Twelfth Annual Report of the Woman's Missionary
Council*, 153.

reported forming committees for undertaking racial work. By the end of the following year, over four hundred were reported. The work was stimulated by a widespread effort to educate the women about the achievements and potential of blacks, current conditions that hindered their progress, and the responsibility of whites both for current conditions and for needed improvement. The goals of the program were accomplished through literature and programs but especially through state and regional conferences held for society leaders. The work of the Methodist women was closely tied to that of the Woman's Division of the CIC. Carrie Johnson was a leading figure in both organizations, and other Methodist women took active roles in CIC interracial work. Methodist women and the CIC often scheduled meetings in the same city so the women could attend both, and Methodist literature frequently contained information about CIC activities.[17]

The nature of the work continued to diversify. As head of the Social Service Bureau, Newell reported that local work for blacks included assuring defendants of a fair trial, investigating school conditions and supporting improvements, assisting in securing loans for building homes, developing recreational facilities, and setting up dental and public health clinics. By the late 1920s, Newell reported that she was encouraged by the growth of the work. She admitted that there remained some of the "widespread indifference" and "positive antagonism" that had beset the early work. Yet she was cautiously optimistic that "there is a slowly rising appreciation of the Negro as a *person* with feelings, with laudable ambitions for education, for a chance to make a good living, and a chance to live in health and self-respect." Only three conferences reported no interracial work, and their areas had very few blacks in the population. The women themselves frequently admitted that they were "changing in their attitude toward this work" and were "growing more sympathetic to the needs" of black people.[18]

17. Dunn, *Women and Home Missions*, 71; *Fourteenth Annual Report of the Woman's Missionary Council*, 135–36. Bennett suggested to MacDonell that deaconesses and others doing interracial work be told simply to ignore any criticism they received (MacDonell, *Belle Bennett*, 124). *Twelfth Annual Report of the Woman's Missionary Council*, 147; *Thirteenth Annual Report of the Woman's Missionary Council*, 130; "Woman's Division, CIC," 108–109.

18. *Fourteenth Annual Report of the Woman's Missionary Council*, 131; *Eighteenth Annual*

As part of the Jubilee Celebration of the council in 1928, the Social Service Bureau sponsored two leadership schools for black women. The project, which had expanded into nine states by 1940, brought together black women for brief periods during the summer in order to provide instruction in both religious and social matters. The teachers, usually some white and some black, conducted classes in child care, sanitation, and nutrition as well as methods for running vacation Bible and church schools. The black women who attended, often given funds by local white auxiliaries, then returned to their local communities to utilize the skills. In 1937 the Colored Methodist Episcopal Church joined in planning and sponsoring these schools, thus giving blacks a more equitable voice in the leadership. [19]

Southern Methodist women also played a major role in the antilynching effort. In 1913, Bennett admonished the women to make known their "disapproval and abhorrence of the savagery that provokes this crime, and by tongue and pen and, in those States where our women have the power of suffrage, by the ballot arouse and develop a public sentiment that will compel a rigid enforcement of the law against such violence until it is no longer known among us." The council supported Bennett's condemnation. The war diverted the women's attention to other matters, but along with their efforts at improved race relations in the early 1920s came a renewed concern about violence and lynching. The women condemned the increasingly influential Ku Klux Klan and applauded the notion that "all Christians should use their voices and utmost influence in suppressing this evil, and in preventing even its inception in American communities." In 1923 the council called on the states to "make good their claim proving their competency to abolish

Report of the Woman's Missionary Council, 142; Seventeenth Annual Report of the Woman's Missionary Council, 120; "Report of Organizations [affiliated with the CIC]" (Typescript in Commission on Interracial Cooperation Papers, Trevor Arnett Library, Atlanta University, Atlanta).

19. Sara Estelle Haskin, "Sharing Our Jubilee," Missionary Voice, XVIII (September, 1928), 23; Jessie Daniel Ames and Bertha Payne Newell, Repairers of the Breach: A Story of Interracial Cooperation Between Southern Women, 1935–1940 (Atlanta, 1940), 7–8; Tatum, Crown of Service, 358–59; Louise Young, "Minutes, Pre-Conference Meeting, CIC, Inc." [April 22–23, 1930]" (Typescript in Commission on Interracial Cooperation Papers, Trevor Arnett Library, Atlanta University, Atlanta).

mob violence and lynching" and urged the women to support efforts to prohibit such acts. This clear antilynching sentiment, however, masked some disagreement over the most desirable approach to eliminating lynching. As an organization, the women had not endorsed the Dyer antilynching bill, killed in the Senate, which provided for federal control of lynching. Many continued to favor local and state control.[20]

As the outburst of racial turmoil and lynchings that characterized the postwar period subsided the leading women of Southern Methodism, along with other southern liberals, were less outspoken. Although the council continued to urge southern politicians to improve protection for prisoners and to make a greater effort to prosecute and convict those guilty of lynching, their demands were less frequent and less urgent.[21]

Yet any quietude in the late 1920s ended with the depression. By 1930, the number of lynchings was again increasing. Will Alexander took the initiative to fight the new trend. With the aid of whites, such as sociologist Arthur Raper at the University of North Carolina, and blacks, such as Fisk sociologist Charles S. Johnson, Alexander developed a number of CIC projects to demonstrate the causes and illegality of lynching and mob violence. Women were, however, not a part of these efforts, and several, such as Mary Downs, who had been active in interracial work protested their exclusion. Jessie Daniel Ames, a Texan who had been extensively involved in both suffrage and interracial work and who had succeeded Carrie Johnson as head of the Woman's Division of the CIC, saw an opportunity to create a woman's organization to protest lynching. This was accomplished in November, 1930, in Atlanta, where a conference of white women, called to discuss increasing violence, formed the Association of Southern Women for the Prevention of Lynching. Southern Methodist women were as significant a force in the new organization as they had been in the CIC. Bertha Newell became secretary of the ASWPL and was one of Ames's closest friends; other leaders including Estelle Haskin and Louise Young, who succeeded Car-

---

20. *Third Annual Report of the Woman's Missionary Council*, 299, 404; Rodney W. Roundy, "Growth of the Ku Klux Klan," *Missionary Voice*, XI (November, 1921), 339; *Thirteenth Annual Report of the Woman's Missionary Council*, 169; "Methodist Women Demand That Mob Violence Be Blotted Out," *Missionary Voice*, XIII (January, 1923), 20.

21. *Fifteenth Annual Report of the Woman's Missionary Council*, 29.

rie Johnson as head of the council's race relations work and who included a course on the Negro in America among her offerings as professor of sociology at Scarritt, also played important roles. A historian of the ASWPL has described the council as the association's "most important endorsing group."[22]

The Methodist women were such a key support for the ASWPL both because they endorsed its objectives and because they provided an organized group that could help attain these objectives. The pamphlets and literature of the ASWPL were frequently distributed through Methodist channels, a substantial amount written by Estelle Haskin. Methodist women by the thousands also signed the ASWPL antilynching pledge and many secured the signatures of law enforcement officers and key political figures as well. The latter efforts sometimes brought the women into open disagreement with their neighbors and family. Many shared the experience of the Methodist woman from Georgia who wrote Ames that her husband, a convict warden in the county, "said he was opposed to lynching unless it was for rape, but I tried to tell him it wasn't right to lynch under any circumstances."[23]

Other disagreements were more public. Dorothy Rogers Tilly, a diminutive Atlanta woman, led a group of women who visited law enforcement officers in two Georgia counties where three lynchings had recently occurred. The women demanded that the guilty be caught and punished. To help ensure that such lax law enforcement did not recur, they also met with and won the support of prominent local citizens and various women's groups. Tilly reflected the spirit that prompted so many of these Methodist women to undertake race relations work. She was a gentle woman who vigorously pursued better social conditions for blacks. Born in southern Georgia in 1883, she was the daughter of a Methodist minister. She graduated from Wesleyan Female College in Macon, as had

22. Hall, *Revolt Against Chivalry*, 161–63, 176; Louise Young interview, February 14, 1972, Southern Oral History Program, Southern Historical Collection, University of North Carolina, Chapel Hill.

23. *Twenty-third Annual Report of the Woman's Missionary Council*; Hall, *Revolt Against Chivalry*, 176; Chairman, Christian Social Relations (Thomaston, Georgia), to Jessie Daniel Ames, February 9, 1934, in Association of Southern Women for the Prevention of Lynching Papers, Trevor Arnett Library, Atlanta University, Atlanta.

Tochie MacDonell, and married Milton E. Tilly, a businessman who shared her concern for blacks and the poor. Beginning her interracial work in the women's mission societies of the Methodist Church, she soon became actively involved in the ASWPL. Her involvement continued well beyond the merger of the MEC,S, with the MEC and the Methodist Protestant denominations. She was active in varied civil rights activities in the 1940s and 1950s, serving on President Truman's Committee on Civil Rights.[24]

The antilynching activities of Bessie Alford of McComb, Mississippi, also demonstrate how Methodist women active in missionary work used that experience for ASWPL work. Along with the help of Ethel Stevens, a Methodist from Jackson, Alford relied on her Methodist contacts to help her form a statewide organization of women opposed to lynching. When violence or lynching threatened, local women could be notified in order to encourage them to take steps to oppose or prevent the action. If local women needed information or assistance, they could rely on the larger network. Like Dorothy Tilly, Bessie Alford had her husband's support for her many activities. She traveled the state, speaking out against lynchings, often addressing women's church groups. She commended sheriffs who protected their prisoners and condemned those who did not. Yet she acknowledged that she encountered considerable opposition. Methodist women could often be noncommittal, and women in other denominations even more so. Her greatest opposition, however, seemed to come from men and often from men in the Methodist Church.[25]

The literature of the Methodist women reflected their close alliance with the ASWPL. Ames, herself a Methodist, warned through the *Missionary Voice* of the dangers mob violence held for basic freedoms in this country. She was convinced that lynchings threatened to undermine the American judicial system. Estelle Haskin, a member also of the ASWPL's

<hr>

24. Clipping from Dallas *Gazette*, July 29, 1933, in Association of Southern Women for the Prevention of Lynching Papers, Trevor Arnett Library, Atlanta University, Atlanta; Dorothy Rogers Tilly Papers, Woodruff Library, Emory University, Atlanta.
25. Bessie [Mrs. L. W.] Alford to Jessie Daniel Ames, July 28, 1938, Bessie Alford to Sheriff Tom Sauls, July 28, 1938, Bessie Alford to Sheriff Brabham, August 4, 1938, all in Association of Southern Women for the Prevention of Lynching Papers, Trevor Arnett Library, Atlanta University, Atlanta; Hall, *Revolt Against Chivalry*, 173, 187, 215–16.

Central Council, used the same periodical to attack the widely bran-
dished idea that lynchings were a necessary deterrent to the would-be
ravishers of southern womanhood. They were, rather, a violation of law
and order and a blight on America and Christianity, at least insofar as
the country claimed to be Christian. Haskin, like many other southern
women opposed to lynching, felt that she had to repudiate those who
claimed that it protected southern womanhood.[26]

The Woman's Missionary Council, meeting in Birmingham, stepped
beyond the ASWPL in 1934, when it endorsed the Costigan-Wagner
Act, which gave federal officials the authority to arrest and try lynchers
when states and localities would not act. The issue of federal control over
lynching had divided southern women for some time. Ten years earlier,
the council had not endorsed similar legislation. Yet by 1934, leaders
such as Louise Young and Estelle Haskin were convinced that federal
intervention was needed. They argued for the legislation before the
council, which registered its overwhelming approval. Such harmony was
not evident in the ASWPL. Ames openly opposed the Costigan-Wagner
Act, arguing that antilynching efforts should be directed toward education and the cultivation of additional local support and suggesting that
enforcement be a cooperative venture between local and federal authorities. Bertha Newell wrote to Ames that she agreed but would not say so
publicly, since the Methodist council had voted the other way. Various
other ASWPL leaders, however, opposed Ames's views, and several resigned their positions. The gruesome killing of Claude Neal, a black man
accused of murdering a white girl, in Marianna, Florida, later in 1934
and the subsequent failure of local officials to issue indictments only further convinced most Methodist leaders that federal intervention was
necessary. Their lobbying efforts failed to convince southern congress-
men, who successfully thwarted efforts to enact such legislation for the
remaining years of the decade.[27]

26. Jessie Daniel Ames, "Whither Leads the Mob?," *Missionary Voice*, XXII (January,
1932), 46; Sara Estelle Haskin, "Southern Women and Mob Violence," *Missionary Voice*,
XXII (February, 1932), 34.
27. Tindall, *Emergence of the New South*, 551–54; *Twenty-fourth Annual Report of the
Woman's Missionary Council*, 34; Bertha Newell to Jessie Daniel Ames, December 18, 1934,
in Jessie Daniel Ames Collected Papers, Southern Historical Collection, University of

In smaller ways also, the women worked to reduce racial tension and ward off violent confrontations. In October, 1930, members of the missionary auxiliaries received a letter from Mrs. F. F. Stephens, Louise Young, Bertha Newell, and others asking them to write to the director of the Association of Motion Picture Producers, expressing the Southern Methodist women's objections to the re-release of the controversial film, *The Birth of a Nation*. The movie was described by the women as containing scenes that fostered racial hatred, and they implied that in its earlier release it had contributed substantially to the subsequent mob violence. Believing the spirit of the film to be contrary to the interracial goodwill for which they labored, mission auxiliary members were urged to oppose its showing.[28]

For over four decades, Southern Methodist women concerned themselves with a vast array of problems that confronted blacks. In the early years of this century, they focused much of their concern on what they perceived to be the lax morality of blacks and the consequences this might have for both races. Nevertheless, they lamented that black women were so often the victims of sexual abuse and deplored the double standard that applied to the females of the two races. Being a group especially interested in strong, stable homes, the Methodist women readily desired "the purifying and uplifting of the negro home." In the context of this concern, they marshaled many of their early efforts to help blacks develop vocational skills and to provide them an admixture of health, sanitation, nutrition, and moral information. It was in a sense the whites' "duty" to blacks, and the women considered themselves especially called to fulfill it.[29]

Tuskegee and Memphis forced many of the women leaders not only to

North Carolina, Chapel Hill; Hall, *Revolt Against Chivalry*, 240–42; *Twenty-fifth Annual Report of the Woman's Missionary Council*, 142–43.

28. Mrs. F. F. Stephens *et al.* to Members of the Missionary Auxiliaries, October 13, 1930, in Commission on Interracial Cooperation Papers, Trevor Arnett Library, Atlanta University, Atlanta.

29. Address of Mrs. B. T. Johnson reproduced in "Woman's Home Missions and the Negro," *Our Homes*, IX (July, 1900), 3; Mary DeBardeleben, "Training for Christian Negro Workers," *Our Homes*, XIX (March, 1910), 11; Lily Hammond, "Our Debt to the Colored Race," *Our Homes*, V (September, 1896), 8–9; "Our Duty to the Negro," *Our Homes*, IX (January, 1900), 1.

recognize that black women shared their concerns but also to appreciate far more profoundly the pain of racism. The aftermath was a major effort to ameliorate the social conditions of blacks, to improve race relations, and to expand the type of work being done. At the urging of leaders like Bertha Newell, Carrie Johnson, Louise Young, and Estelle Haskin, thousands of local societies surveyed their communities to determine conditions for blacks, and many, worried by what they found, lobbied for better schools, housing, health care, and other reforms. Antilynching work was only among the most visible of their activities. What, though, were the major ideas that the women brought to this work? What were the specific attitudes they held toward blacks? What were the fundamental ideas that governed their actions, and how did these develop during the decades of their interracial activities? The evidence reveals that the women were influenced by an interplay of religious and cultural factors.

The women most active in home mission work in the Methodist Episcopal Church, South, were convinced that the region's racial problems could be solved by applying to them the ideas and teachings of the Christian religion. In fact, they believed that no merely secular solution would ever prove satisfactory. Because of this certainty, they were disturbed by the widespread hostility and the indifference of the church. Addressing a gathering of Methodist ministers in 1910, Belle Bennett suggested that "if the seven thousand itinerant preachers in Southern Methodism could be divested of their prejudice against the Negro . . . the [racial] problem would soon be solved." Lily Hammond complained similarly that "the pulpits of the South rarely speak of those problems which press upon us all, and for which there is no solution outside the teachings of Christ." Louise Young remarked, decades later, that it was "a mystery" to her why the church had not pressed more strongly for better relations between the races.[30] Christianity, the women believed, commanded race relations work.

These statements should not hide the fact that the women were aware and supportive of the efforts to improve the social conditions of blacks that some men in the church and the South made throughout the early

30. MacDonell, *Belle Bennett*, 126; Hammond, *In Black and White*, 210; Young interview, February 14, 1972, in Southern Historical Collection.

decades of this century. Certainly, the women cooperated with the efforts of Bishop Charles Galloway and, later, Will Alexander. Yet Methodist women were convinced that they also had a major role to play in improving race relations. Around the turn of the century, they witnessed black disfranchisement and Jim Crow laws in the South, signs of a virtually complete segregation of the races. Physical violence and race-baiting gave rise to increasing antagonism. In 1903, Lily Hammond wrote that it was widely known "that many Southern people hope for no solution of the negro problem which will allow the negro to remain in the South on friendly terms with his white neighbor." Such "impatient or despondent" people could think of no ultimate resolution of the race problem, save voluntary or forced colonization or the natural extinction of blacks because of their contact with a "higher civilization." But she wrote that, along with a growing number of others, she held a different view. They were not, she noted, unmindful of the "negro's needs and deficiencies." These she regarded as "too near at hand and too clamorous to be overlooked or mistaken." Yet, unlike others, Hammond and her comrades would not acquiesce to the idea that what was, was inevitable. Their differences with most southern whites were not over the present but over the future. The achievements of many blacks, exceptions to the general condition, caused them to "draw from the acknowledged facts more hopeful conclusions than [did] their neighbors." They had attached their faith to the idea of progress.[31]

The commitment in this century's early years of Lily Hammond and other women leaders of Southern Methodism to progress for blacks was generously mixed with a firm conviction that such progress could best be attained through help from a presently superior white race. After the Memphis conference, talk of the relative development of the races would virtually cease, but it was a significant motivating factor in the early work among blacks. "The more they need our help as Christians," Lucinda Helm wrote, "the more incumbent upon us is the duty of lifting them up." Her sister, Mary, warned that, although blacks could sometimes do more effective mission work among their own race than could

31. Lily Hammond, "A Southern View of the Negro," *Outlook,* LXXIII (March 14, 1903), 619.

whites, the time had not yet come for whites to cease helping "nor will it come until we have done still more to develop this 'backward race,' which by a strange providence has been placed in the reach of our help-ing hand." The council's Social Service Bureau, chaired by Lily Ham-mond, considered it an obligation "to arouse the women of our auxil-iaries to a sense of their personal duty as Christian Southerners, to meet the needs and ameliorate the conditions of those of this backward race who are in their midst by personal service and sympathy." [32]

Not surprisingly, therefore, the council urged members at its 1915 meeting to help black women form their own mission societies. It was each member's "duty to act as counselor and advisor to the colored women." Confident of their own developed superiority, they were equally confident that the assistance they provided blacks would have beneficial results. "The finest and strongest Negroes, I believe without a single exception," wrote Lily Hammond in *In Black and White*, "have come to their high development largely through contact with broad-minded, large-hearted white men and women." [33] Without arrogance, the leading women of Southern Methodism believed that they were such persons.

Mindful that they lived in a post-Darwinian age and influenced by the widespread religious ideas of their day, the women saw the world as dy-namic and capable of evolving toward a better state. The black man as part of that world could share in that progress. It made no sense to the women to condemn a whole race to perpetual deprivation. The black race was fully capable of improvement. Even the women's most patroniz-ing statements contained this faith. In her 1903 article in the *Outlook*, Lily Hammond claimed that "it would be difficult to exaggerate the lack of morals among the mass of the negroes." Still she concluded that "the

32. Lucinda Helm, "The Negro Problem," *Our Homes*, VI (September, 1897), 3; Mary Helm, *The Upward Path: The Evolution of a Race* (Cincinnati, 1909), 289; *Third Annual Report of the Woman's Missionary Council*, 403.

33. *Fifth Annual Report of the Woman's Missionary Council*, 144; Hammond, *In Black and White*, 203-204. Hammond apparently accepted the idea that more informed and priv-ileged women have a unique responsibility for social morality. She argued that "racial adjustment, like many other moral issues, waits on the leadership of these women" (Ham-mond, *Southern Women and Racial Adjustment*, 5).

whole human race has come up from the depths in this respect; and, remembering how recently their forefathers were savages, the situation is not without encouragement."[34]

The women believed that the course of history gave foundation to their hope for the black race. Mary Helm acknowledged that she had spent the "greater part" of her book, *From Darkness to Light*, presenting facts that "show the processes of the evolution through which the Negro has passed from the African savage to the Christian citizen of America." When she revised the book, on its recommendation by the interdenominational Council of Women for Home Missions, she changed the title to *The Upward Path: The Evolution of a Race*, thus conveying her message more explicitly. From such a viewpoint, she could present a temperate apologetic for slavery. While not arguing that the system itself was good, she believed that "with its discipline and training [it] was the first great step in the evolution of the African savage into a citizen of civilization." This conviction she coupled with a defense of the Southern whites who had been unfairly maligned for bearing this "burden that none but themselves understood."[35]

Lily Hammond was less sanguine about slavery but no less certain of black development. In the opening chapter of *In the Vanguard of a Race*, a book also used for the study program of the Council of Women for Home Missions, she traced the rise of Anglo-Saxon civilization from barbarian beginnings to twentieth-century accomplishments. By outlining the development of whites, she hoped to convince them that the black race was likewise capable of future achievements. The major focus of the book, however, was the recounting of the lives of blacks of outstanding achievement. It was this group of "exceptional" black men and women that the women of Southern Methodism pointed to as convinc-

34. Hammond, "A Southern View of the Negro," 620.
35. Mary Helm, *From Darkness to Light: The Story of Negro Progress* (2nd ed.; New York, 1909), 13; M. Helm, *Upward Path*, 34, 41. In the period of racial tension in the early years of this century, some of the women shared the tendency to romanticize race relations during the slavery period. The current mistrust and hatred were unfavorably compared with the perceived harmony and closeness of an earlier era. See "A Dual Work," *Our Homes*, XV (January, 1906), 1. Woodward, *Origins of the New South*, 352–55, points out that the caste system that replaced slavery in the South was widely acknowledged, even among blacks, to have made race relations worse.

ing proof that the race itself was capable of substantial accomplishment. Hammond declared that she hoped to persuade her readers, most of whom would be white women like herself, "not only [to] respect the achievements of to-day and yesterday, but [to] see them as foreshadowings of the possibilities of a people." A similar sentiment led Estelle Haskin to prepare study books that included brief biographies of successful black Americans for the society's youth auxiliaries. The women were convinced that it was "in these exceptional negroes, and in their constantly, if slowly, increasing numbers, that we find a visible warrant for our faith in the future of their race, as well as for our faith in the providence which has bound up their future with that of the whole country." [36]

The women of Southern Methodism viewed human history as a progressive continuum. Their own white race had developed far along the scale and, though not without significant shortcomings, had constructed a praiseworthy civilization. Blacks were also in this continuum, though many of the women, particularly in the early years of this century, were inclined to see them as much lower on the scale. Yet in a real sense, the women always tended to believe that the direction in which the race was moving, or was capable of moving, was as important as where it was. Many considered Reconstruction an unfortunate period for whites and blacks and believed that blacks were asked to assume more responsibility than they were capable of shouldering. They regretted the animosity and hatred that characterized the post–Civil War period and moved into the new century. [37] Despite these difficulties, the women were convinced, the history of blacks in America and the achievements of notable individual blacks were strong evidence of the possible progress of the race.

Yet perhaps more significant, they believed that progress itself was the cornerstone of the divine plan for human history. Blacks were a part of God's providential plan of "ultimate success for the whole human race."

36. Lily H. Hammond, *In the Vanguard of a Race* (New York, 1922), 15; Sara Estelle Haskin, *The Handicapped Winners* (2nd ed.; Nashville, 1925), and (assisted by Rebecca Caudill) *The Upward Climb: A Course in Negro Achievement* (New York, 1927); Hammond, "A Southern View of the Negro," 621.

37. M. Helm, *Upward Path*, 80, 83; Hammond, "A Southern View of the Negro," 621–22.

Mary Helm argued that "by His hand the life of humanity in its development is directed step by step ever towards Himself." Such sentiments were expressed not to minimize the human role but to suggest the seeming inevitability of an improving and happy future. If most of the Methodist women were usually less certain of the inevitability of progress, they were no less convinced than Helm of its probability if they cooperated with God's work and followed his command. Tochie MacDonell wrote that, for Belle Bennett, "progress was the law of life." Therefore, MacDonell continued, "she believed in the progress of the whole Negro race. . . . The genius of her faith in the establishment of God's kingdom on earth made her work unceasingly, regardless of race inheritance to bring that day 'when all mankind is perfected, equal in full bloom.'"[38] Southern white women had been assigned a major role in bringing blacks into the growing kingdom.

For the women, it followed logically that if progress were possible for blacks, improving their environment would make it a reality. Mary Helm believed that blacks in America had "through a new environment escaped many retarding conditions, and passed with unnatural rapidity through processes of evolution that have left the race as a whole far behind." Writing in the first decade of the twentieth century, she thought that "the industrious, educated Christian Negro offers no problem to-day, and when the race has passed through these processes of education and industrial training there will be no problem for the future."[39] She shared a view widely held among women of Southern Methodism that the poverty, ignorance, and immorality that they perceived as widespread among blacks could be largely cured with a good dose of social improvements, education, and gospel.

The women were slow to abandon their own sense of superiority,

38. Mrs. Frank P. Smith, "The Education of the Negro in the South," *Missionary Voice*, IV (June, 1914), 382; M. Helm, *From Darkness to Light*, 202; MacDonell, *Belle Bennett*, 124–25. Bennett's courage and progressive thinking are reflected in a story set in her own Madison County, Kentucky. Before a scheduled address by W. E. B. Du Bois, Bennett learned that a small area had been roped off for the exclusive use of whites. She immediately had the rope removed and said that anyone could sit in that area (MacDonell, *Belle Bennett*, 137).

39. M. Helm, *Upward Path*, 4; M. Helm, *From Darkness to Light*, 14.

though the work of the early 1920s would alter this perception for many. Yet even prior to this, they began to appreciate the fact that black people were victims of the environment in which they lived. "In this reasoning, scientific age, when we have come to know the subtle yet tremendous influence of environment over character," Mary DeBardeleben pointed out, "we cannot consistently censure the laxness and shiftlessness among many negroes until we have done all we can to better their housing conditions." That DeBardeleben was serving as the first Southern Methodist woman to labor as a settlement worker among blacks gave her words added significance. Lily Hammond argued similarly that poor housing for blacks was a cause of other social problems they faced. Southerners, she noted, were inclined to consider these poor living conditions "an outward and visible sign of an inward racial lack, not realizing that conditions such as we provide for them breed physical and moral degeneracy wherever furnished, in people of every race the world around." The poverty of blacks, she contended, was a result not of some racial flaw but of the political system. Black slums were attributable to the same causes as other slums. They were all "the joint product of ignorance, greed, and the monstrous old doctrine of *laissez faire*." [40]

A year later, Hammond presented a similar argument in the *Christian Advocate*, the denomination's major periodical. She contended that southerners had been too quick to believe in the black's "inborn, ineradicable tendency toward crime." Rather, she pointed out, evidence indicated that better home environments reduce the amount of crime among black youths. [41]

In view of their emphasis on the importance of environment in explaining the condition of blacks, it is not surprising that the women most active in home missions would encourage study of these conditions, with an eye toward reform. In race relations, as in other home mission work, attention was increasingly focused on eliminating the causes of social ills rather than merely treating the symptoms. The council supported the

40. Mary DeBardeleben, "Opportunities for Service Among the Negroes," *Missionary Voice*, II (April, 1912), 209; Lily Hammond quoted in unsigned editorial, "Better Housing for Negroes," *Missionary Voice*, III (August, 1913), 459; Hammond, *In Black and White*, 94.
41. Lily Hammond, "Light on Negro Delinquency," Nashville *Christian Advocate*, LXXV (October 16, 1914), 26–27.

efforts of scholars and educators who conducted "scientific investigations" of the social and legal situation of blacks. After establishing local
committees to support interracial work, the women themselves conducted investigations and supported efforts at reform. These efforts were,
after all, beneficial to whites as well as blacks. Bertha Newell reminded
the women in the local auxiliaries that the destiny of blacks was closely
tied to that of the South and its white population. The health, economics, and morals of one race influence those of the other.[42] The influences
of environment affected everyone. In the South, all profited from the
efforts to better the living conditions of blacks.

The women's attitudes toward the black person were mitigated not
only by their conviction that he was to a significant extent a creature of
his environment. Their attitudes were also transformed by their developing awareness that he was also a creature of God. Faithful to their Methodist tradition, the women had always held an inclusive rather than an
exclusive theology; that is, they believed that everyone was both created
by God and was able to be saved. It was understood that this idea applied
to the black as well as the white. Thus each person, regardless of race,
was of great value. For Southern Methodist women, this value could not
be restricted to one's spirit. They were convinced that God cares about
all persons and all parts—physical and mental as well as spiritual—of
each person. This fundamental faith was a major stimulus to the women's
attitudes toward and work among blacks.

"Everybody on earth," Lily Hammond wrote, "is human first and racial
afterwards. We must see in the Negro first of all, deeper than all, higher
than all, a man made in the image of God as truly as we ourselves."
There was a solidarity about the human race, a truth that racial antagonism overlooked. It was "God's law," Mary DeBardeleben told the society's members, "that underneath the outer differences we *are one*."[43]
Environmental interdependence had a religious dimension as well. The
economic and spiritual intimacy between blacks and whites was part of a
divine plan that made human concern for the neighbor imperative.

42. *Third Annual Report of the Woman's Missionary Council*, 274; Bertha Newell, "Negro
Leadership," *Missionary Voice*, XVI (September, 1926), 27.
43. Hammond, *In Black and White*, 87–88; Mary DeBardeleben, "The Missionary Society: October Program," *World Outlook*, XXIV (September, 1934), 25.

For the women, the increasing importance of the idea of human solidarity necessitated a reevaluation of their attitudes toward blacks. If each
person were a creature of God, then each held enormous value. The
Commission on Race Relations declared that, if the race problem in
America were to be solved, all persons must be recognized as "children of
God" with a chance to realize the potential of their lives. It held that
"sacredness of personality is the basis for all civilization, [and] it cannot
be expected that any race can purify itself, raise its standards, and fit into
the life of a nation as a valuable asset instead of a liability and menace
while held in contempt and ridicule and . . . patronized as mendicants."
The commission spoke in 1924. The following year Carrie Johnson,
deeply moved by her experience as head of the commission and the
Woman's Division of the CIC, cautioned the society's members not to
forget that, in the long history of organized mission work among women
in the denomination, the nation had "not only been unjust to a race of
people in her power, but has practiced barbarism, which is scarcely sur-
passed by any of the most barbarous and pagan peoples of the world."[44]

The words reflected a dramatic change in attitude among the women
most active in the interracial work. The sense of racial superiority so
evident in the women's attitudes in the early years of this century was
gradually giving way to a new respect not only for what the black might
become but also for what he presently was. Carrie Johnson believed that
no race could call itself superior "as long as the man who is strong intimi-
dates and terrorizes the weak."[45]

The practical experience of some of the women in interracial work
also helped to change attitudes. Mary DeBardeleben admitted that she
had begun her work among blacks "with the decided feeling of superiority." Yet she reported that, during her years of work in Augusta, she

44. Fourteenth Annual Report of the Woman's Missionary Council, 136, 139; Mrs. Luke
[Carrie] Johnson, in Fifteenth Annual Report of the Woman's Missionary Council, 133. Similarly, George Tindall ("The Central Theme Revisited," in Charles G. Sellers [ed.], The
Southerner as American [Chapel Hill, N.C., 1960], 119–20) has suggested that the ill-
treatment of blacks has often been at odds with the American idea of the individual's
essential worth. Although not assigning social Christianity a large role in southern religion, he also suggests that the region's religious consciousness created some uneasiness with
regard to oppressive racism.
45. Johnson, in Fifteenth Annual Report of the Woman's Missionary Council, 133.

came to an "appreciation of what was good and true and beautiful in the Negro race and to a sense of shame and humility for having been so blind and dumb as not to understand more readily." Reflecting on the history of the work in 1931, Mary Downs, known for a certain gruffness and directness, concluded that she could perceive this new respect for blacks. Over the years, she wrote, the women "became aware, they could hardly tell how, of an increasing consciousness of the hurt and wrong of racial prejudices, and through a period of years of contact and cooperation they have grown to know that 'races were not superior one to another, but that some of them have been less favored by circumstances.'"[46]

However, the question remains whether this growing respect for blacks was accompanied by a desire for more integration of the races. Certainly around the turn of the century, the South was experiencing increasing segregation in practically all areas of life. Schools, theaters, trains, waiting rooms, and water fountains were only a few of the places that had fallen prey to Jim Crow. Although the women of Southern Methodism lamented the absence of friendly and instructive contacts between blacks and whites that they imagined had been prevalent in an earlier day, they rarely objected to the social and political division of the races. What they regretted was the effort on the part of many whites to use the fear of interracial mixing, or "social equality," to stir the flames of racial antipathy and to make the condition of blacks worse.[47]

Such social mixing or "equality," the women believed, was no more desired by intelligent blacks than by whites. Lily Hammond argued that the "better class" of blacks did not want it. Such mixing she considered impossible in the immediate future, though "this fact does not prevent mutual kindliness nor respect." She commended Booker T. Washington

46. DeBardeleben quoted in Channing H. Tobias, "Two Southern Women Pioneering," *World Outlook*, XXII (October, 1932), 29; *Twenty-first Annual Report of the Woman's Missionary Council*, 79; Thelma Stevens interview, February 14, 1972, Southern Oral History Program, Southern Historical Collection, University of North Carolina, Chapel Hill.

47. By his denial of "social equality" to blacks, the southern white was calling for segregation in all areas of life. This included what Gunnar Myrdal (*An American Dilemma: The Negro Problem and Modern Democracy* [2 vols.; New York and London, 1944], I, 60–61) described as the greatest fear of southern whites—racial amalgamation. Harold Lloyd Fair, "Southern Methodists on Education and Race, 1900–1920" (Ph.D. dissertation, Vanderbilt University, 1971), 291–302.

for showing both blacks and whites how "to live side by side in justice and friendship" while maintaining that they should remain "in things purely social as separate as the fingers, yet one as the hand in all things essential to mutual progress." Bertha Newell added that "neither right-thinking whites nor self-respecting Negroes desire any form of social equality and will wisely oppose any efforts to bring it about." Most of the women would readily have agreed that "the right-minded negro desires social distinctions between the races quite as much as does his white brother."[48]

Therefore, the whole issue of social equality, the women frequently reiterated in the first quarter of this century, was merely a false issue that served to exacerbate racial tensions and justify the ill-treatment of blacks. The *Missionary Voice* reprinted a selection from the Southern Publicity Committee, which Lily Hammond established to disseminate favorable accounts of black accomplishments, decrying "the mistaken belief that educated Negroes desire social relations with white people." These blacks, the writer argued, wanted to make it clear to their own race as well as to whites "that they are satisfied to be Negroes; that they believe that Negroes, and Negroes only, can furnish what Negroes want in home and social life." The issue was in fact settled in the thinking of the "best" members of both races. For Mary Helm, social mixing of the races was not really the focus of the problem but a "mirage that has led to false standards and disappointed hopes and then been used as a club to beat them back from the end sought after."[49] It was, in other words, a diversion from achieving real progress.

Real progress was understood as the economic, educational, and moral advance of the black race. Unlike many southerners, Methodist women

48. Washington's remarks are taken from his famous 1895 address to the Atlanta Cotton States and International Exposition. His "Atlanta Compromise," which was widely accepted in the black community for many years, identified black interests with industrial education and economic opportunity rather than with political rights or social privilege. Woodward, *Origins of the New South*, 357–60; Hammond, "A Southern View of the Negro," 620; Hammond, *In the Vanguard of a Race*, 27; Bertha Newell, "Race Relations at Young People's Convention, Memphis," *Missionary Voice*, XVI (March, 1926), 30; "The Black Man in America," *Missionary Voice*, IV (November, 1914), 601.

49. "Negro Education and 'Social Equality,'" *Missionary Voice*, X (March, 1920), 92; Mary Helm, "My Neighbor," *Our Homes*, XVII (August, 1908), 7.

active in the early years of interracial work took seriously the idea of "separate but equal." They sought not the intermingling of the races but the uplift of black people. As difficult as it might have been for some whites to accept, the women were convinced that most blacks wanted only improved sanitation, better housing, and equal justice. Bertha Newell argued that, when blacks sought housing closer to white residential areas, the motivation was improved living conditions and not racial mixing. "Negroes, like white people," Lily Hammond concluded, "like to live among their friends."[50] Yet they liked to live among their friends in a decent environment, and this the women of Southern Methodism believed that they deserved.

This belief seemed grounded in a viewpoint part secular and part sacred, though the women did not clearly distinguish between the two. The cornerstone of a democratic government, they contended, was equality of opportunity. They recognized that the conviction that each person should have the opportunity to advance, and the supporting notion that each held that potential, conflicted with a society that afforded one race inferior facilities and limited possibilities. The women were not revolutionaries, and the reforms they supported to improve conditions for blacks were frequently seasoned with both gradualism and condescension. Yet many of them in a real sense were visionaries, and the vision they held included the possibility for each person to realize his or her potential. They recognized that such a vision had never been a reality but believed it to be "a part of Christ's will for man and . . . fully included in the meaning of the petitions, 'Thy kingdom come; thy will be done, as in heaven so on earth.'" A society that valued all its members and helped them realize their worth had a distinctly religious dimension. However halting the progress toward such a society, the end sought was "the realization of human brotherhood and the kingdom of God on earth."[51]

50. Bertha Newell, "Housing the Negro," *Missionary Voice*, XV (November, 1925), 22; Hammond, *In Black and White*, 126.
51. "Making Democracy Safe," *Missionary Voice*, IX (February, 1919), 50; Lily Hammond, "The Growth of Democracy in the South," *Methodist Quarterly Review*, LIV (January, 1905), 37.

Yet the question remained whether such a goal was compatible with a racial doctrine of "separate but equal." Was the kingdom of human brotherhood a place of racial distinctiveness? The women's ambiguous answers to this largely unformed question reflected the tension between the tenets of the culture in which they lived and those of the ideal society for which they were striving. As their repudiation of social equality indicates, the leaders of the women of Southern Methodism frequently expressed their support for racial separation, in the first quarter of this century. Mrs. W. J. Piggott, a member of the original Commission on Race Relations, urged blacks and whites to march into the future "in a spirit of friendly cooperation" and yet "in separate companies." Lily Hammond assured her readers that progress for the black race would not lead to more interracial mixing. "Life does not develop towards uniformity," she wrote, "but towards richness of variety in a unity of beauty and service. . . . What we white people need to lay aside is not our care for racial separateness, but our prejudice." [52] Frequently, the women maintained that what they wished was more not less race consciousness, integrity, and self-esteem.

However, their position was not wholly consistent. The women seemed unmindful of the likely conflict between urging blacks to develop their own racial integrity and at the same time insisting that blacks accept the women's instruction and values. Yet if the implications of their efforts often escaped them, they were not unaware of the shortcomings of a segregated kingdom. Southerners, the *Missionary Voice* reflected, were "keenly alive to the necessity of social separation, [yet] without doubt we need a broader vision of the oneness of our human community problems and the oneness of our Christian obligations." Mary Helm acknowledged that, although the social relations between the races had been settled in the "narrow" sense, the "broader" meaning of the Christian's obligation to his neighbor remained largely unexplored. Although she endorsed social distinctions between the races, Lily Hammond considered them "superficial and temporary." There was only one true distinction in the world, she told the annual meeting of the North Georgia Conference

52. *Sixth Annual Report of the Woman's Missionary Council*, 132; Hammond, *In Black and White*, 44.

Society, the one that separated "the class that serves God and the class that serves him not."[53]

Planted within the women's theology were the seeds that would gradually weaken their loyalty to racial separateness. The conviction that each person, regardless of race, was valuable and worthy of concern mixed uneasily with the idea of "separate but equal," particularly when such conditions did not exist. The women of the Methodist Episcopal Church, South, never fully resolved the tension. It was not until after World War II that Southern Methodist women would join other Methodist women, with whom they were then united in a single denomination, to call publicly for integration of society's major institutions.[54]

Yet in the interwar period, the expressions and activities of many women of Southern Methodism underwent change. The mission workers who worked at one of the Bethlehem Centers, such as Estelle Haskin in Nashville and Thelma Stevens in Augusta, lived in a world populated largely by blacks. Stevens noted that the first three years she was in Augusta, she was isolated from the white community. Louise Young was the only white faculty member and one of only three whites on campus when she went to Paine College in 1919 and reflected later that she was living in an almost totally black world. Such circumstances did not necessarily create close or equal relationships with blacks. Stevens and her white coworker acquiesced to community opinion and roomed in a building separate from the black coworkers, though they all took the radical step of eating together.[55]

During the 1930s, there was further evidence of cooperation. More and more local auxiliaries reported that they had worked cooperatively with groups of black women in their communities to resolve common problems, and many individual women sought advice on setting up interracial programs for community improvement. In response to a letter from Miriam Rogers of Clayton, Georgia, seeking such counsel, Jessie Daniel Ames encouraged the creation of a community welfare club and Bible

53. "Black Man in America," 601; "Our Duty to the Negro," *Our Homes*, XIX (March, 1910), 1; Hammond, "Our Debt to the Colored Race," 2.
54. See Stevens, *Legacy for the Future*, 60–65.
55. Stevens interview, February 14, 1972, Young interview, February 14, 1972, both in Southern Historical Collection.

study class as a joint venture of the Methodist Missionary Society and the nearest black mission society. Clubs like this one would examine the economic, social, and educational conditions of local blacks. Moreover, Bertha Newell reported that many members had studied *A Preface to Racial Understanding* by Fisk sociologist Charles S. Johnson and had acquired from it new insight about racial prejudices. The leadership training schools that the council had sponsored during the summers since 1928 became jointly sponsored with the black women of the Colored Methodist Episcopal Church in 1937. The condescension so evident in the early sessions diminished as black women assumed more leadership roles. All of these point to increasing contact and cooperation between the races on a more equal basis.[56]

The leaders of the interracial work reflected this changing attitude in their response to the unification of the Methodist Episcopal Church, South, with the Methodist Episcopal Church and the Methodist Protestant Church. The council's Committee on Interracial Co-operation, under the leadership of Louise Young, called the plan to set aside a separate jurisdictional conference for most black members of the new church "less than ideal." The committee concluded that the scheme left "much to be desired if the Methodist Church is to represent fully the Kingdom of God on earth" and expressed its regret that the new church would be virtually segregated below the General Conference level. Nevertheless, the committee's women recognized the barriers to better race relations. "Our churches as a whole," they regretfully agreed, "are not yet ready" for more interracial cooperation; perhaps the present solution was the best possible under the circumstances.[57]

Probably more than any other single area, the women's work in race relations manifested tensions between social norms and religious ideas. Their activities and opinions reflected the influence of both, yet they never drew a distinction between the two. They believed that Christian teachings could resolve the problems between blacks and whites in the

56. Jessie Daniel Ames to Miriam Rogers, August 28, 1936, in Commission on Interracial Cooperation Papers, Trevor Arnett Library, Atlanta University, Atlanta; *Twenty-seventh Annual Report of the Woman's Missionary Council*, 116–17.
57. Louise Young, "Unification and Race Relations," *World Outlook*, XXVII (June, 1937), 29–30; *Twenty-seventh Annual Report of the Woman's Missionary Council*, 140–43.

South, and they were convinced that white women had a major role to play in the solution. Underlying all of their work was the conviction that blacks, like all people, were capable of progress. The course of history and the achievements of individual blacks confirmed this belief. Such progress was predicated, however, on a changed environment. Black people, the women believed, were victims of poor social conditions. If blacks were to advance, their living conditions must improve. They must have good schools, decent housing, strong families, and adequate job opportunities. The women believed that their Christian mission included working for such improvements.

A perspective that understood environment as the key to progress stimulated social reform activities, but it did not always beget respect for the beneficiaries of those activities. The early years of this century found the Methodist women often announcing the superiority of whites and the necessary social separation of the races. But the passing years largely tempered this view. Loyalty to the convictions of God-given individual worth and human solidarity helped create the possibility for interracial respect and cooperation, a possibility that was enhanced by increasing interracial activities.

Although Christians across the country called for improved race relations in the interwar period, the issue inevitably posed a greater challenge for the social Christianity of the South. The women of Southern Methodism active in home missions, joined by other southern men and women, responded to what they perceived as their Christian obligation. In part, they were tied to many of their society's racial ideas, but they were also emboldened and changed by the teaching and practice of their faith. They believed that black people as well as white were a part of the earthly kingdom they were seeking to extend. Religion, so often society's captive, itself influenced the course of the women's interracial work.

Chapter V / *Extending the Kingdom to Women*

For the mission workers of Southern Methodism, the kingdom of God required recognizing the worth of women as well as that of blacks, immigrants, and the poor. The increase of home mission activities coincided with and profited from the expanded role of women in America in the late nineteenth and early twentieth centuries. Although white women in the antebellum South had had their influence largely restricted to the home, conditions in the period after the Civil War were conducive to women's pursuing a broader social role. Those in the middle and wealthier classes found themselves with increased leisure time. No longer responsible for overseeing slaves, they were also confronted with a large population of black women who of necessity performed housework for very low wages, which released white women from those chores. Improved technology, particularly evident in growing cities and towns, served as well to reduce household demands. Many women in urban areas increasingly were exposed to the varied ideas of newspapers, magazines, and books that resulted from improvements in various areas of communication. All these factors contributed to the creation of a group of southern white women living in closer proximity to one another, more aware of the world beyond their local communities, with leisure time for undertaking whatever activities they might choose.[1]

Social conditions were the foundation of the growing tendency toward activism among southern women; a deep discontent with the unfamiliar world of the late nineteenth century was what stirred them to ac-

---

1. See Eleanor Flexner, *Century of Struggle: The Woman's Rights Movement in the United States* (Cambridge, Mass., 1959). A less optimistic appraisal of women's progress is provided by William L. O'Neill, *Everyone Was Brave: The Rise and Fall of Feminism in America* (Chicago, 1969). A more complete discussion of the prevailing social conditions can be found in Anne F. Scott, *Southern Lady*, 227–31, and "Women, Religion, and Social Change in the South, 1830–1930," in Samuel S. Hill, Jr. (ed.), *Religion and the Solid South* (Nashville, 1972), 102.

tion. Many concurred with Caroline Merrick, an active worker for the Woman's Christian Temperance Union in New Orleans, who reflected that women were "tossed to and fro amidst the exigencies and bewilderments of strange and for the most part painful circumstances, and were eager that new adjustments should relieve the strained situation, and that they might find what to do." Perhaps uncertain of what to do to lessen the social dislocation, racial tension, and immorality they perceived around them, the women believed that the church was the institution through which they could realize the new adjustments. Here women were permitted more freedom of action than in other social institutions, largely because many men viewed church work as suitable for women and as "no compromise of female modesty and refinement." Numerous women joined missionary societies in Southern Methodism and other denominations. Active participation in the church was "the essential first step in the emancipation of thousands of southern women" from a sphere of influence and work limited to the home.[2]

Thus, the social situation of the South gave many white women leisure time, and the church provided an opportunity for women to invest their time and resources. The church permitted the women's organizations, through which they came to a greater appreciation of their abilities and self-worth. This new confidence and altered self-understanding were essential in encouraging the women to seek greater authority and independence in the denomination.[3] In addition, the church provided the women of Southern Methodism with specific ideas about their mission and worth as women that stimulated the active work they pursued.

Two convictions spurred many Southern Methodist women to greater mission activity: that women, as well as men, had been given the divine command to extend the kingdom of God on earth and that women, in addition to men, were fully members of the kingdom, inherently as worthy, as valuable, and as able. There were three specific struggles in which the issue of women's proper role in the Southern Methodist

2. Caroline E. Merrick, *Old Time in Dixie Land* (New York, 1901), 172; A. W. Plyler, *The Iron Duke of the Methodist Itinerancy*, quoted in Scott, "Women, Religion, and Social Change," 109; Dykeman and Stokely, *Seeds of Southern Change*, 143; Scott, *Southern Lady*, 135–44.
3. Scott, "Women, Religion, and Social Change," 109–110.

Church was paramount: the merger of the home and foreign missionary societies, women's right to serve the church in all capacities open to male lay members, and women's right to be ordained to the church's clergy. The debate over the issues reflects the importance of religious ideas to the women's understanding of their proper function in the church.

The women's struggle to realize an expanded role in the MEC,S, does not seem to constitute home mission work if it is defined in a narrow sense. However, if only because the struggle was a major element of the total mission work and was integral to the implementation of other mission projects, one should consider it here. Moreover, the women's struggle for recognition within the denomination was grounded in many of the same religious convictions that motivated the rest of their work; their arguments in favor of the granting of women's laity rights in particular were often couched in terms of a further extension of the kingdom of God. As they labored to bring others, such as immigrants and blacks, into the kingdom it was necessary to carry on a concurrent struggle for denominational recognition of their rights.

The idea promulgated by the mission societies that women shared with men the God-ordained responsibility to spread the kingdom of God on earth clashed with the traditional belief that woman's proper sphere of responsibility was limited to the home. Yet the women of Southern Methodism were firmly convinced that their religious obligation extended to the world around them. Speaking to the 1893 annual meeting of the society's North Mississippi Conference, the president, Nellie Nugent Somerville, reminded the women that they belonged "not only to one family, but to the great human family. Motherless humanity needs your womanly care. Then let your sympathies widen, thank God for your freedom, accept the opportunity, and help in this work." Somerville rejoiced that the sympathies and activities of a woman no longer had to be "limited by the walls of her own home." This socially imposed restraint denied the fundamental religious truth of human oneness. God's followers, she believed, had been commissioned to serve all people. A year later, Mrs. C. O. Jones welcomed members to the Louisville Conference Home Mission Society annual meeting with a reminder of the new opportunities and responsibilities they faced. She rejoiced that "the world [is] open to our word and waiting for help." She prayed that God would help the women perceive the privilege of their obligations.[4]

Many Southern Methodist men found it difficult to accept the idea that woman's responsibilities went beyond the home. There is substantial evidence to support the conclusion of Hunter Farish that generally in the late nineteenth century "the Methodist Episcopal Church, South, maintained traditional views with regard to the position of women in society." Major spokesmen for the denomination often denounced women's suffrage and only somewhat grudgingly endorsed the activism among women burgeoning in their own church. Mrs. F. F. Stephens, council president, concluded in 1925 that the records of the early years of mission work "fail to show any marked enthusiasm on the part of the Church at large for the new member of the official family." Women's mission activities, she observed, challenged traditional theories "about the ability of women to think, plan, and work." In a similar vein, Maria Gibson, longtime president of Scarritt, closed a session of the council's Executive Committee in 1926, which had considered a problem with the Board of Missions, with a prayer recalling the difficulty some men had created for the women's work in the early days: "Dear Lord, we pray for the men of the Board of Missions. Thou knowest how they have troubled and worried us. They have been hard to bear sometimes, but we thank thee that they are better than they used to be."[5]

Despite the attitude of most Southern Methodist men regarding the proper sphere of women's activities, there were signs of change. Farish acknowledges that, in contrast to his general conclusion, some evidence existed "of a willingness to grant woman a more dignified position in the Church and to concede to her a broader sphere of activity in society at

---

4. [Sara] Estelle Haskin, "Women as Lay Members—What Will It Profit?," Baltimore and Richmond *Christian Advocate*, IX (February 24, 1910), 2; "Address of Mrs. Robert [Nellie] Somerville, President, at the Annual Meeting of the North Mississippi Conference," *Our Homes*, II (August, 1893), 3; Mrs. C. O. Jones, "Welcoming Address," *Our Homes*, III (April, 1894), 6.

5. Hunter Dickinson Farish, *The Circuit Rider Dismounts: A Social History of Southern Methodism, 1865–1900* (Richmond, 1938), 325–26; *Fifteenth Annual Report of the Woman's Missionary Council*, 49–50; Gibson, *Memories of Scarritt*, 131–32.

large." The General Conference did sanction the establishment of both foreign and home missionary societies for the women. Here the women profited from the tendency of many Methodist men to grant them considerable freedom to pursue their own church activities; the women enjoyed substantial autonomy. In addition, they received the active support of some men such as David Morton, secretary of the Board of Church Extension. A few men were joining a growing number of women in rejoicing in the "new woman . . . whose heart has been freed and fired by the religion of Jesus Christ, and whose hands are busy in the blessed work of lightening and lifting the burdens of others."[6]

Southern Methodist women active in mission work were participating in a gradual redefinition of a woman's proper social role. Their conviction that God had called women to assist in extending the kingdom to the world was a challenge to the image—widely held in the South—of the ideal woman as gentle, submissive, morally pure, and concerned only with matters of the home and family. The Methodist women saw the "ideal" society member as a person who carefully attended to her home and who sought also to understand, care about, and aid the social situation of others in her community and beyond. The charity she showed toward her family she now shared with others in the broader world, and her passive acceptance of social realities gave way to a determination to alter them.[7]

Addressing the opening session of the 1912 meeting of the council, Belle Bennett noted that fifty years previously the ideal mother focused her love predominantly on her own children. Now, she argued, the ideal mother, though of course caring for her family, extended her concern to suffering women and children wherever they might be. Almost two decades later Estelle Haskin reiterated the importance of Christian women's taking an active role in relieving social problems. There was, she wrote, a growing belief that offering only money and prayers for a social problem did not completely fulfill the responsibility of a Christian woman. She

6. Farish, *Circuit Rider*, 326; "Col. [George] Thornburgh's Address," *Our Homes*, VI (January, 1897), 1.

7. "The Ideal Member of a Missionary Society," *Our Homes*, VII (November, 1898), 3; see Anne F. Scott, "After Suffrage: Southern Women in the Twenties," *Journal of Southern History*, XXX (1964), 299; Scott, *Southern Lady*, 4–21.

was convinced that "an enriched life giving itself for the kingdom on earth is the final and only real offering that can be adequate or can satisfy." She believed that a mission organization should help an individual live such a life and rejoiced that the women had "evolved from a female cent society to an organization the ideal of which is, 'Every member an evangel of the new social order.'"[8]

Southern Methodist women were certain that God intended for them to be colaborers with men in the task of spreading the kingdom on earth. In fact, some of the women indicated their belief that women had a unique responsibility for social reform. The woman's section of the *Missionary Voice* editorialized that members of the local missionary auxiliaries were frequently the persons most aware of a community's social needs. These women were, it maintained, "by reason of the vision which has come to them, the God-appointed leaders and promoters of the new mission of the Church of God." Similarly, Carrie Johnson argued that "there is no force so great in shaping the future citizenship of Church and State as is that force called womanhood." Belle Bennett's greatest contribution to the world and to the church was, according to her biographer, "the womanhood which she stimulated with a passion for the kingdom of God."[9]

Southern Methodist women rejoiced that their sex was rightfully taking its place as a full participant in the divine task of spreading the kingdom. They believed that women brought special capacities to the effort. Bennett maintained that the sexes were equal, but she denied that they were identical. Woman had her distinct contribution to make. Mission activists may have challenged the image of woman as socially passive, limited in her concerns to the home, but they reinforced and developed the idea of woman as compassionate and idealistic. Members were reminded that women's "genius for cherishing ideals" was their greatest power; they had "a special knowledge of suffering and love" that expressed itself in unselfish concern for others. Women were less materialis-

8. *Second Annual Report of the Woman's Missionary Council,* 8; Sara Estelle Haskin, "The Recent Council Meeting," *Missionary Voice,* XX (May, 1930), 37.
9. "Social Service Undergoes Important Changes," *Missionary Voice,* X (June, 1920), 178; *Twenty-second Annual Report of the Woman's Home Mission Society,* 94; MacDonell, *Belle Bennett,* 160.

tic and more sensitive to human needs than were men. The Methodist women insisted that the feminine hope for a more compassionate world be coupled with personal involvement. Winifred Kirkland, in an article entitled "God Is Waiting for Women," applauded the fact that Christian women were combining their vision of religious truth with a "stern strain" of practical help for the world's problems. Mary DeBardeleben held up Dorcas, who served the needy in the early church, as a model for missionary women—"to the poor a helpful, faithful friend at all times; to the women a leader; to the Church a dynamo of power and strength."[10]

Therefore, the idea that women were commanded by God to assist in extending the kingdom moved easily into the corresponding notion that God had created women as persons as able and worthy as men. The council's Committee on Research and Study of the Status of Women argued that the "Christian woman is called by God to serve him and for that reason he endowed her with talent, ability, capacity, and she shall render unto him an account of her stewardship."[11] Many of the women of Southern Methodism came to understand that view. They were convinced that Christianity taught the worth and value of each person, and they perceived that this idea commended an expanded social role for women.

The leaders among Southern Methodist women certainly were not blind to the problems that Scripture often posed for their increased activity. They knew that a literal interpretation of many biblical passages had been used to restrict women's place in the church and society. The use of the writings of Paul was of special concern. Mrs. W. J. Piggott, an active social service worker, lamented the fact that "the behavior of the church has been influenced by literal interpretations of Paul's writings on many matters more than by the teachings of any other in the New Testament." Leaders like Mary Helm and Mary Moore made it clear that they

10. Belle Bennett, "The History of the World-Wide Movement for the Liberation of Women," *Methodist Quarterly Review*, LXI (January, 1912), 58; Bertha Conde, "Adult Auxiliaries—October: If Jesus Came To-day, Would We as Women Recognize Our Debt to Him?," *Missionary Voice*, XVI (September, 1926), 28; Winifred Kirkland, "God Is Waiting for Women," *World Outlook*, XXII (April, 1932), 31; Mary DeBardeleben, "Bible Study," *Missionary Voice*, I (June, 1911), 51.
11. *Twenty-fifth Annual Report of the Woman's Missionary Council*, 159.

believed that many of Paul's teachings concerning women were cultur-
ally conditioned and did not apply to the present day. Helm concluded
that the resulting double standard in the church, which Paul's teachings
had encouraged, had created "more injustice, suffering, and sin than any
other evil that the world has accepted, an evil that in the end is more
hurtful to the moral and spiritual life of men than of women." [12]

Rejecting a rigidly literal application of particular biblical passages,
the women of Southern Methodism active in mission work were in fact
certain that fundamentally the Scriptures supported a fuller and freer role
for women. They sharply differed with the conclusion of Elizabeth Cady
Stanton and a few other feminists that the Bible and Christianity were
major stumbling blocks to the equality of women. The antagonism of
Stanton and other feminists to the Bible and the church led in the 1890s
to their issuing the *Woman's Bible*, a two-part commentary on the Scriptures. Some passages were cited by the various authors as evidence proving that the Bible hindered the progress of women; other passages were
interpreted to indicate that they described woman as man's equal. In
general, however, Stanton, who headed the project, was quite hostile to
the Bible. Atticus Haygood's denunciation of that radical position was
endorsed by the *Our Homes* readership. [13]

In contrast to Stanton, the mission women argued that the Christian
message rightfully interpreted and correctly applied had been and would
continue to be the central liberating force for women. The "dominant
note of Christianity, even in its lowest forms," Belle Bennett maintained, "has been a note of liberty." She saw the efforts in her own day
for progress for women as "distinctly and insistently the results of the
teachings of Jesus Christ, and the operation of the Holy Spirit upon the
hearts of men." She believed that throughout Christian history, when
the church had been truly faithful to the message of the Founder, there

12. Mrs. W. J. Piggott, "If Christ Make Us Free," *Missionary Voice*, XXII (March, 1932),
21; Mary Helm, "Why Not?," *Our Homes*, XIX (January, 1910), 5; Mary N. Moore, "Shall
Our Methodism Accord Women the Privileges of the Laity?," *Methodist Quarterly Review*,
LXII (October, 1913), 738.

13. Aileen Kraditor, *The Ideas of the Woman Suffrage Movement, 1890–1920* (New York,
1965), 75–95; Atticus Haygood, "The Cady Stanton Bible," *Our Homes*, IV (August,
1895), 2–3.

had been "a corresponding advance in the social, economic, and educational status of women." [14]

The women perceived the life and message of Jesus as the foundation that supported their progress. They believed that "when Christianity has been true to the teachings of its Founder, women are neither put up on a pedestal nor looked down on as inferior: they are viewed simply as persons and are treated with the regard to which persons are entitled." Piggott noted Jesus' "absolute disregard of any difference in the spiritual ideals, the spheres, and potentialities of men and women." This attitude, she held, derived from Jesus' belief that "the individual had an infinite value in the eyes of God; therefore, a right to consideration and respect from men." Quite simply, Jesus valued all persons because God did, and he refused to limit or look down on women. From them, he anticipated the realization of the gifts God had granted them. The Committee on the Status of Women concluded that Jesus "gives to men and women an abundance of life which permits and expects development of full personality." [15]

The women were convinced that, where Jesus' message of individual worth and mutual respect and love had taken hold, the condition of women had improved. Without explicitly denying that the church had sometimes proved an obstacle to the progress of women, they nevertheless agreed with Mary DeBardeleben "that wherever the Christ has been able to make his way to the hearts of men, amelioration of woman's burdens has been the result." Southern Methodist women saw a direct link between the spread of Christianity and the growth of the woman's movement. Mary Moore wrote in 1913 that woman's advancing place in the world was "in truth a by-product of the great missionary movement." Christian women, she pointed out, had assumed new responsibilities through their missionary activities, and the status of women in America and other countries had been improved because of the impact of Christian missions. "In the stillness of our souls," Mary Helm suggested to

14. Bennett, "History of the World-Wide Movement," 54.
15. Albert Barnes, "The Missionary Society: The Indebtedness of Women to Jesus," *World Outlook*, XXVIII (May, 1938), 33; Piggott, "If Christ Make Us Free," 21; *Twenty-second Annual Report of the Woman's Missionary Council*, 161.

mission workers, "let us contrast woman in this Christian land with what she was before Christ came, or where he is not known today."[16]

Thus, for these Southern Methodist workers, consideration of the role of women was inextricably linked with Christianity. They believed that God had commissioned women as well as men to help extend his kingdom in the world. In addition, he had done what his commission implied—created both women and men as worthy and able individuals with potential for serving him that should rightfully be utilized. Women, in other words, were to be fully accepted members of the kingdom they sought to build. The leaders of the women's mission movement in Southern Methodism saw Christianity, not as a hindrance to, but as the primary authenticator of an expanded role for women. The essence of Christ's life and message demanded that women assume larger responsibilities.

The Southern Methodist women did not view themselves as identical with males; in fact, they emphasized women's special sensitivity and social and moral concern. Nor did they consistently call for complete equality with men in all areas of church work or in positions of authority. Although they were continually supported by the belief that God wished them to work for a kingdom in which they were to be fully accepted citizens, their particular application of the belief developed over the years. The new roles they assumed and asked to assume grew gradually.

Three issues most clearly focused the struggle of Southern Methodist women for recognition within their own denomination: the merger of the women's foreign and home missionary societies, laity rights for women, and clergy rights for women. Through the arguments that passed back and forth on all sides of these issues, one can discern the support the women found in their religious convictions as well as the opposition they encountered from both men and women. In all cases, they attempted to ensure a wider participation for women in the life of the church, a situation they considered consistent with the divine will.

The struggle over the merging of the foreign and home missionary

16. Mary DeBardeleben, "Adult Bible Lesson—December: Jesus the Friend of Burdened Womanhood," *Missionary Voice*, XV (November, 1925), 28; Mary Moore, "The Influence of Christianity on the Position of Women," *Missionary Voice*, III (November, 1913), 657–58; Mary Helm, "Christ, Our Blessing," *Our Homes*, VIII (December, 1899), 1.

societies dramatically revealed to the women the lack of authority they held in the Methodist Episcopal Church, South. By the turn of the century, the women of Southern Methodism had built strong foreign and home missionary societies, separate from one another and largely independent of male control. In 1906 this structure, which had proved satisfactory to the women, was directly challenged by the General Conference, the denomination's highest governing body.

The opening salvo in the dispute came when the all-male Board of Missions and the College of Bishops recommended to the General Conference that the women's two missionary societies be united and that the new organization be brought more directly under the control of the Board of Missions. The women had not been consulted about the proposed changes, and most learned of them only through press reports a few days prior to the session's opening. As news of the preemptory move spread, the Woman's Board of Home Missions, which was holding its annual meeting in Asheville, North Carolina, moved quickly to authorize its president and general secretary, Belle Bennett and Tochie Mac-Donell, to attend the conference and "act for the Woman's Board of Home Missions in promoting its interests." The women were surprised and saddened by the proposals. Bennett acknowledged to the other home mission leaders that "this may be our last meeting." She urged the women to pray for guidance for themselves and for the men of the General Conference, where women "have neither voice nor vote, part nor lot." [17]

Bennett and MacDonell moved on to the General Conference, meeting in Birmingham, where they were joined by Mrs. A. W. Wilson and Mrs. J. B. Cobb, officers of the Woman's Board of Foreign Missions. Here the women encountered difficulty finding an audience to hear their concern. Not only were women not permitted to serve as delegates, they were denied the privilege, save by special permission, of speaking on the floor or in committee meetings. Thus, the four women were largely reduced to assisting male delegates sympathetic to their plight and lobbying delegates outside the formal meetings.

17. Tatum, *Crown of Service*, 29; *Twentieth Annual Report of the Woman's Home Mission Society*, 36; MacDonell, *Belle Bennett*, 232, 233–34.

The women made it clear that they did not disagree with the stated intention of the leading men of the church to establish a closer relation among the denomination's various boards, thereby eliminating unnecessary bureaucracy and duplication. What they did object to was the men's failure to hear and incorporate the ideas of the women who would be most affected by the change and who would likely have the most practical and workable solutions to the problem of multiple organizations. Moreover, the women clearly differed with many of the men over the form the solution should take. The bishops and the Board of Missions had recommended that the new united organization be placed under the authority of a predominantly male board. Bennett and MacDonell, representing the Home Mission Society, suggested that all the church's mission work be placed under the authority of a general board or council, composed equally of men and women. "So foreign," Bennett recalled, was the idea of equal representation "to the time-honored policy of Methodism that the mere formal announcement of the bill met with a good-humored ripple of laughter."[18]

The women's resistance to the proposed union did, however, influence the action of the General Conference. Although the Committee on Missions reported that such a union "is eminently to be desired," it recommended, and the conference concurred, that a commission be established to study the issue and suggest the most desirable method of achieving that union. The conference proposed that a commission of thirteen, nine men and four women, be selected to undertake the assignment and report their findings to the 1910 General Conference.[19]

Although the issue was unresolved, the momentum was overwhelming for uniting the two women's organizations and placing the newly formed body under closer control of a general board of missions. The women could only hope to maintain as much independence as possible for their new organization. They pressed hard for their case. The Woman's Home

18. *Twenty-first Annual Report of the Woman's Home Mission Society*, 31–32; MacDonell, *Belle Bennett*, 233–36. Thirty years later, the Methodist Church—into which the Methodist Episcopal Church, South, had merged—granted women half the membership on the Board of Missions, excluding the positions held for active bishops. See Sara Estelle Haskin, "Women and the New Methodist Church," *World Outlook*, XXIX (July, 1939), 12.

19. *Journal of the Fifteenth Session of the General Conference*, 201–207.

Missions Board argued that for the "best interests of the missionary work of the Church this organization should maintain its present autonomy." Belle Bennett warned that "any disturbance of the Woman's Missionary Societies . . . will bring about such a disturbance of relationships in the Church as Methodism has never known."[20]

The women viewed the end result with very mixed emotions. After months of disagreement, the thirteen-member commission finally reached consensus on a plan at its final meeting prior to the 1910 General Conference. The proposed plan, which the conference ratified without amendment, merged the two women's boards into the Woman's Missionary Council, while permitting the local and conference home and foreign societies to remain separate. The council was placed under a board of missions of thirty-nine elected and seventeen *ex officio* members, with fifteen of the total number being women, although the council retained considerable autonomy in many areas including finances. Although home and foreign societies were not required to merge under the 1910 General Conference action, the council recommended that they begin taking such steps. Many readily complied, and, in 1914, union became constitutionally required at all levels.[21]

Despite some concessions to their desire for independence, the women were not enamored of the new structure. Yet because they perceived that a more favorable plan was not forthcoming—in fact, they feared a worse one—most endorsed it. The four women who served on the Unification Commission, Maria Gibson, Belle Bennett, Tochie MacDonell, and Mrs. J. B. Cobb, issued a statement to General Conference delegates declaring their belief that most women would accept the commission's plan and suggesting that the delegates not seriously amend it. Yet the four remained mindful of "the distress and agitation that the passage of this paper will bring to the one hundred thousand women whom we represent." Gibson, in fact, had only agreed to sign the commission's report after she became convinced that lack of unanimous support from

20. *Twenty-third Annual Report of the Woman's Home Mission Society*, 40, 48.
21. Tatum, *Crown of Service*, 30, 33–34; Haskin, *Women and Missions*, 33–34; *Daily Christian Advocate*, XVII (May 9, 1910), 34; statement to General Conference delegates, reprinted in *Our Homes*, XIX (June, 1910), 1; Gibson, *Memories of Scarritt*, 162–63.

commission members might lead to amendments even more damaging to women. Belle Bennett also apparently grudgingly accepted the compromise. She wrote Mrs. F. F. Stephens that she "did not believe in the union of the Woman's Board with the General Board on the basis which we were compelled to accept." She agreed, she wrote, because she feared something worse—"complete subordination." [22]

A few women refused to accept the changes. Margaret Polk, a physician who did medical missionary work in China, was so angered by the proceedings that she withdrew her membership in the Methodist Episcopal Church, South. The Executive Committee of the new Woman's Missionary Council expressed sympathy with Polk's feelings but urged her, apparently unsuccessfully, to reconsider. Further strenuous opposition came from Mary Helm, a dogmatic opponent of union, who announced sadly that "Belle has sold her birthright" and resigned her long-held position as editor of *Our Homes* in protest. She perceived the new Woman's Council as dominated by the male Board of Missions and contended that "thus we are completely deprived of our autonomy and all administrative powers." "We are," she wrote to Nellie Somerville, "in a helpless minority in a body where the membership is largely made up of men opposed to independence of thought in women." [23]

However, most of the women were determined to continue active mission work within the new organization. A number of leaders suggested that the changes brought not only new challenges but certain advances. MacDonell and Cobb argued that, rather than removing responsibility from the women, the union meant "increased opportunity and larger life." Missionary women, they maintained, now had not only "the past autonomy of the auxiliaries and conference societies, but through their representatives have part in the general administration of missionary interests of the church." Bennett and Gibson also stressed the significance of having female representation on the Board of Missions, so women

22. MacDonell, *Belle Bennett*, 143; statement to General Conference delegates, 1.

23. *First Annual Report of the Woman's Missionary Council*, 47–48; Mary Helm to Nellie Nugent Somerville, August 29, 1910, in Scott, *Southern Lady*, 142, and in Shadron, "Out of Our Homes," 73–75; MacDonell, *Belle Bennett*, 145. The periodical that Mary Helm and her sister, Lucinda, had guided for over eighteen years was, under the new agreement, to be merged into a general missionary periodical, the *Missionary Voice*.

would have "a voice in the whole missionary policy of the Church." MacDonell praised the elimination of "the dividing lines of home and foreign missions" and welcomed the new "opportunity of concerted action between the men and women of the Church in the mission fields."[24]

Therefore, most women leaders combined public enthusiasm for the new organization with private dismay at what they perceived to be the men's high-handed tactics. Yet the women's predominant feeling, expressed both publicly and privately, was one of genuine concern over the future of their work. "We naturally face the future," Bennett told the initial meeting of the council, "with mingled feelings of hope and fear." Despite their apprehensions, the women moved quickly to make the new organization harmonious and effective. The officers and executive committees of the two woman's boards met together within a few days of the action of the General Conference and elected new officers. The following year Belle Bennett, the council's first president, led the members in their first annual session. Thus the women began a successful new organization that, in the thirty years of its existence, was to eclipse the combined size and scope of the two groups it replaced. As Bennett surveyed the first four years of the united work in 1914, she appeared genuinely satisfied with the accomplishment. The change had necessitated sacrifice and pain, she concluded, but, overall, the work had prospered. She was particularly pleased that women and men had worked cooperatively in directing the mission activities of Southern Methodism. Other Protestants, she noted with enthusiasm, were carefully watching this joint effort and were coming "to see in it another enlarging of the kingdom of God on earth."[25]

The struggle over their missionary organizations, however, made the women acutely aware of their powerlessness in the Methodist Episcopal Church, South. They saw that women were doing much of the work of

24. Mrs. R. W. [Tochie] MacDonell and Mrs. J. B. Cobb, "The Board of Missions and the Woman's Work of the Church," *North Carolina Christian Advocate,* LV (August 4, 1910), 6; Belle Bennett and Maria Gibson, "A Message to Our Colaborers," *Our Homes,* XIX (July, 1910), 1; Mrs. R. W. [Tochie] MacDonell, "The Woman's Board and the Board of Missions," *Our Homes,* XIX (July, 1910), 4.

25. *First Annual Report of the Woman's Missionary Council,* 96; Haskin, *Women and Missions,* 35–37; *Fourth Annual Report of the Woman's Missionary Council,* 74–75.

the church without comparable authority to influence the denomination's policies. As she had with so many projects, Belle Bennett assumed the initiative in tackling this problem. Addressing the 1909 meeting of the Woman's Home Missions Board, Bennett urged the members to petition the General Conference to grant women "all the rights and privileges of the laity" of Southern Methodism. The basic thrust of her proposal was to gain for women the opportunity to serve as voting members in the decision-making bodies of the denomination. Pointing out that the women of Northern Methodism had had similar privileges for twenty years without "great calamity," she maintained that granting women additional authority would benefit the entire church. She supported the plea with Paul's words in Galatians 3:28, a passage that was to become one the women quoted most frequently: "There can be neither Jew nor Greek, there can be neither bond nor free, there can be no male and female; for ye are one in Christ Jesus." [26] Although other parts of the Bible, especially the Pauline letters, served as ammunition for her opponents, Bennett's selection of her text is evidence of her belief that, rightly understood, the biblical message was the foundation of the women's quest for equal rights in the church.

Seeing that the proposal would be unpopular in the church at large, the board nevertheless voted, twenty-nine to six, to support Bennett's recommendation to seek from the 1910 General Conference "the full rights and privileges of the laity" for the women of the church "that they may help to hasten more surely and speedily the coming of the kingdom of God." Carrie Johnson was appointed to head the drive to seek conference approval. [27]

The action by the board set off a sometimes acrimonious debate that soon overshadowed the consideration of the union of the women's organizations. Although the arguments, which waged back and forth as three separate General Conferences considered the question, were often more emotional than insightful, they largely centered on four general issues.

The most fundamental issue was that of woman's proper role, particu-

26. *Twenty-third Annual Report of the Woman's Home Mission Society*, 48–49.
27. MacDonell, *Belle Bennett*, 239; *Twenty-third Annual Report of the Woman's Home Mission Society*, 163.

larly as the Bible prescribed that role. As was indicated earlier, the women saw the Bible as conveying the message that God intended woman for a freer, more expanded social role than she held in the early twentieth century. However, many men and women in Southern Methodism, also relying on biblical passages, claimed that woman's God-ordained role was far more limited. The debate over laity rights for women brought the two conflicting opinions into sharper focus.

Writing in the *Christian Advocate*, the Reverend H. T. Allen condemned the movement for laity rights, reminding women that their proper sphere was the home. He complained that "our dear women ought not to want so much" and warned them to "remember the fate of poor Eve, who took a little more than God intended for her to have." E. C. Reaves, a layman in the church, agreed that men and women were ordained by God to work in different spheres, with women's primary sphere being the home. He opposed laity rights for women because "a female, strutting in the garb of masculinity, takes on boldness in lieu of modesty . . . and loses that delicate yet all-commanding influence she cannot carry beyond her orbit immutably fixed in the beginning." Similar sentiments about God's designated division of labor between the sexes were voiced by delegate George R. Stuart at the 1910 General Conference. Woman's work was of great importance, he acknowledged, but he pleaded with his fellow male delegates to "let her work in her field, and let us work in our field." [28]

The women who led the fight for laity rights and their supporters were equally convinced that God had not circumscribed women's limited sphere of influence and activity. God had, in fact, commanded them to share fully with men the task of fulfilling the divine purpose in the world. Addressing the 1910 annual meeting of the Woman's Home Missions Board, held just prior to the General Conference, Bennett acknowledged that it would be "infinitely easier and more comfortable to let some one else interpret the will of God for us, and fix our 'sphere.'" She also admit-

28. H. T. Allen, "Laity Rights for Women," Nashville *Christian Advocate*, LXXV (May 1, 1914), 555–56; E. C. Reaves, "Equal Rights and Privileges with the Laity," Nashville *Christian Advocate*, LXXI (April 15, 1910), 470; "General Conference Proceedings," *Daily Christian Advocate*, XVII (May 20, 1910), 118.

ted that "some will even be able to prove from the Bible that women have no scriptural right" to work to improve social conditions beyond their own homes. Yet, Bennett thought, an understanding that the Christian message limited the role of women was wrongheaded. Christ had granted each person the fundamental freedom to do his will and to realize his or her potential. She lamented that now, in considering woman's rightful place in the work of the church, so many, male and female, had substituted the "traditions of men" for the liberating word of God. Most of the women mission leaders shared the opinion, voiced by a man, that "the gospel of Christ is responsible for the 'women's question.'"[29]

Inevitably, the issue of laity rights for women intensified the debate within the Methodist Episcopal Church, South, over the limits of female participation and authority. As Bennett so fully appreciated, the request was itself a challenge to social tradition. Yet for both sides, it was also a fundamental religious question of how God had ordered the world and of what tasks had been assigned to his creatures.

A second issue often argued in the debate over laity rights was its impact on the participation of men in the life of the church. Both sides agreed that the active involvement of men was desirable and both regretted that more men were not presently engaged in the various phases of the church's work. However, they disagreed on what the male's disinterest in religious matters implied for the laity rights of women.

Those who opposed laity rights argued that granting women this additional authority would only cause men to assume less responsibility. J. M. Barcus, a Texas clergyman, pointed out that the women of the church already had much work to do and need not be burdened with more. Yet, he maintained, if men had the possibility of giving women more work, they would do so. The granting of laity rights to women would only permit men to spend more time "making money." Although more positive than Barcus on the work being done by the men of Southern Methodism, the Reverend W. F. Evans of Arkadelphia, Arkansas,

29. *Twenty-fourth Annual Report of the Woman's Home Mission Society*, 40–42; A. M. Trawick, Jr., "Woman's Representation," Nashville *Christian Advocate*, LXXI (February 25, 1910), 8–11.

shared his conviction that granting women greater authority would lessen male efforts. He warned the women to curtail their request "lest the white heat of consecrated manhood be cooled and the kingdom of our Christ suffers."[30]

The concerns of the men were shared by some women who opposed the granting of laity rights. Writing in the Nashville *Christian Advocate*, an anonymous member of the Home Mission Society maintained that passing the proposal would mean less work by men. A somewhat similar conclusion was reached by Mrs. J. W. Perry, second vice-president of the Woman's Board of Home Missions and one of the few women leaders who opposed the movement to win laity rights at the 1910 General Conference. She maintained that women should welcome exemption from this burden that men were presently bearing. She asked the women to let men continue to do this particular work and argued that the mission work had never been hindered by the women's lack of laity rights, contending that their influence through husbands or sympathetic males had more impact than that which a few women delegates to conferences would wield. The opposition to laity rights by this officer of the board was significant, if only because it added strength to claims by male opponents that most women did not wish laity rights.[31]

The proponents of laity rights for women saw the issue quite differently. They maintained simply that women should be permitted the authority to help influence those policies of the denomination that they were already working to carry out, as a matter of justice. "What long-suffering creatures women are anyway," wrote Nellie Somerville. "They consent to hold office in a sort of *sub rosa* way, doing all the hard work; but as soon as some immature stripling or reformed drunkard joins the Church he gets the office, while the women keep on doing the work."

30. "General Conference Proceedings [1910]," 116; W. F. Evans, "Lay Women or Not?," Nashville *Christian Advocate*, LXXI (April 29, 1910), 531.
31. "Woman's Representation," Nashville *Christian Advocate*, LXXI (April 1, 1910), 407–408; Mrs. J. W. Perry, "The Memorial of the Woman's Home Mission Board," Nashville *Christian Advocate*, LXXI (April 15, 1910), 475–76; Lily Hammond, "The Rights of the Laity," *Our Homes*, XIX (July, 1910), 7; Mrs. J. W. Perry, "Why the Women of the Church Do Not Want the Rights of the Laity," *Southern Christian Advocate*, LXXIII (February 24, 1910), 2–3.

Tochie MacDonell shared similar thoughts. If, she contended, women were doing much of the work in the educational and mission programs of Southern Methodism, then they should have the right to serve on the church's decision-making bodies. Mary Moore agreed and noted that to deny these women workers the opportunity for laity rights was to deny the church the value of their experience and expertise. What the supporters wished was not a system that granted special privileges to women but one that was blind to their gender and aware of their merit. Some women, Somerville warned, have "reached the limit of patience," watching church work "directed by careless, unspiritual men, while faithful, pious women are kept in the background."[32]

The proponents of laity rights also appealed on occasion to the special sensitivities attributed to women. Mary Helm noted that "on every side we hear the lack of spiritual life in the Church deplored. We hear also the assertion that women are more spiritual, more devout than men. Is not something left out that Christ intended to be in the management and councils of his Church when the spiritual female element of that Church is excluded from its directing and controlling offices and councils?" To Helm, female laity rights were crucial to creating the balance Christ intended in the leadership of the church.[33]

Two additional issues in this controversy were voiced less often but were also a vital part of the general debate. One issue centered on whether the proposal for laity rights for women was part of a broader movement to win privileges for women in and out of Southern Methodism. The opponents assumed the offensive by labeling the women who supported the proposal "suffragettes" and secret advocates of female ordination to the clergy. That many men feared that granting women laity rights would create a domino effect is seen in an exchange over the issue between two clergymen during the floor debate at the 1910 General

32. Nellie Somerville, "The Church and the Women," *Our Homes*, XIX (February, 1910), 25; Mrs. R. W. [Tochie] MacDonell, "Why Women Ask the Rights of the Laity," Nashville *Christian Advocate*, LXX (November 19, 1909), 24–25; Moore, "Shall Our Methodism Accord Women the Privileges of the Laity?," 735; Haskin, "Women as Lay Members," 2; Somerville, "The Church and the Women," 23.

33. Mary Helm, "Shall Right Yield to Opposition?," Baltimore and Richmond *Christian Advocate*, IX (March 17, 1910), 11.

Conference. N. B. Henry noted that "no man can even cursorily read history in the light of what Christianity has done for women, and not realize that in the course of time (and that time is pretty near full), she will not only come into possession of all that she asks in this memorial, but of very much more." "That," E. M. Glenn replied, "is what we are afraid of." The *Daily Christian Advocate* recorded that Glenn's remark was followed by "great applause."[34] This domino theory was popular among many who opposed laity rights for women.

Some of the women leaders did express their individual support for granting females the political vote, either through the church press, as did Belle Bennett, or through membership in groups that promoted women's suffrage. Mabel Howell and Tochie MacDonell, for example, were both members of the Nashville Equal Suffrage League; Nellie Somerville was president of the Mississippi Woman's Suffrage Association from 1908 to 1912 and the first female legislator in Mississippi. A survey of prominent Southern Methodist women in 1914–1915 reveals that 60 percent favored women's suffrage while only 10 percent opposed it.[35]

Nevertheless, attempting to combat the effects of the argument that laity rights were a mere first stepping-stone on a seemingly endless road of female demands, the women were often forced to deny that laity rights had any relationship to political voting or to clergy rights. As was noted previously, Southern Methodist women, as an organization, remained virtually silent on the suffrage question. Women's suffrage, Mary Helm contended, was a "personal matter," and she argued that the action of the Home Missions Board to petition the General Conference for laity rights should not be considered an endorsement.[36]

The leaders of home mission work issued an even stronger denial that the campaign for laity rights was a disguised action whose real goal was ordination to the clergy. They echoed Helm's declaration that the move-

34. John M. Barcus, "Woman's Rights in the Church," Nashville *Christian Advocate*, LXXI (April 1, 1910), 391; Allen, "Laity Rights for Women," 555; "General Conference Proceedings [1910]," 116.
35. Bennett, "History of the World-Wide Movement," 54–72; Shadron, "Out of Our Homes," 13, 80–81.
36. Mary Helm, "A Correction with a True Statement," *Our Homes*, XVIII (November, 1909), 3.

ment for laity rights "was no covert plan to possess ourselves of the rights of *clergy*. That one naturally develops into the other is an absurd argument." That women would seek clergy rights two decades hence is no evidence that these women were involved in subterfuge. Rather, their effort to focus the discussion on the issue of laity rights, and only laity rights, indicates their sensitivity to the political necessities of the situation.[37]

The second issue that often surfaced in the debate was the degree of support enjoyed by the petition among all the women of the denomination. The opponents announced repeatedly that the movement for laity rights had the support of only a small percentage of the church's women. The request to the 1910 General Conference, the Reverend John Barcus declared, did not represent the wishes of most Southern Methodist women. It had not been endorsed unanimously by the Woman's Home Missions Board; the organization as a whole had taken no vote on it; and he argued that most of the church's women were not even members of the Home Mission Society. George R. Stuart concurred with Barcus in 1910 that most women did not desire the legislation. He claimed that only 8 of the 140 local home mission auxiliaries in his conference had voted to support the change; others had either voted against it or shown so little interest that no vote at all was taken. It is of note that Mrs. E. E. Wiley, one of the mission leaders who did oppose laity rights, was from Stuart's conference.[38]

However, the men's arguments did not reflect the support that did come from many quarters. Endorsements came from numerous conference home mission societies as well as scores of district and local auxiliaries. Clergy and laymen joined thousands of women in signing petitions of support. Yet, ultimately, the women did not wish to base their case on numbers. They were willing to acknowledge that many Methodist women did not support laity rights but contended that such opposition came most frequently from women who had little experience in church work and thus little awareness of the need for official representation in

37. Mary Helm, "Laity Rights for Women," *Our Homes*, XIX (May, 1910), 5.
38. Barcus, "Woman's Rights in the Church," 391; "General Conference Proceedings [1910]," 118.

church decision-making bodies. The question of laity rights, they maintained, should be decided, not on its popularity, but on its merits.[39]

Despite an active campaign by the women, the 1910 General Conference did not grant their request for laity rights. The bishops, noting what they believed to be majority sentiment, opposed the change and were supported by approximately two-thirds of the male delegates. However, the women found reason for encouragement even in the defeat. The matter had been given serious consideration and had received considerable support from many males. The General Conference delegates had granted Belle Bennett privileges of the floor to present the case for laity rights, the first time in the denomination's history a woman had addressed a conference session. Carrie Johnson interpreted events optimistically, reporting that "we have been agitating this question only six months; hence we feel that a great victory has been ours in that the question was so quickly placed before the Church, that the attention of bishops and preachers was so surely secured, that the committee which passed upon it gave it careful consideration . . . and that a woman was permitted to speak for women before that great body."[40]

In 1910 the women of Southern Methodism who supported laity rights believed that the course of history was moving in their direction. They understood that rarely did radical changes take place quickly. If women were to secure increased authority in the church, extensive educational work was needed. Women, as well as men, had to be persuaded of the justice and significance of an expanded role for women. Continued struggle was the prescription; supporters would not "cease nor abate any effort until this work of righteousness is accomplished."[41]

However, the accomplishment of laity rights for women would have to wait almost another decade. Despite widespread lobbying efforts on be-

39. Mary Helm, "The Memorial of the Woman's Board," Nashville *Christian Advocate*, LXXI (April 15, 1910), 469; Tatum, *Crown of Service*, 38–39; *Journal of the Sixteenth Session of the General Conference*, 269; M. Helm, "Shall Right Yield to Opposition?," 4.

40. *Journal of the Sixteenth Session of the General Conference*, 26, 267–69; MacDonell, *Belle Bennett*, 241–42; Mrs. Luke [Carrie] Johnson, "The Woman's Memorial," *Our Homes*, XIX (June, 1910), 23.

41. Belle Bennett, in *Twenty-fourth Annual Report of the Woman's Home Mission Society*, 39.

half of laity rights, the 1914 General Conference also voted against the proposal, by a wide margin. The bishops reaffirmed their opposition. Although Belle Bennett was again granted privileges of the floor to speak on behalf of the proposal, similar privileges were given Mrs. T. B. King of Memphis, a critic of laity rights. The conference's action suggested that most of the men present appreciated King's contention that "we want to be womanly women, with all the sweetness and the gentleness that God has endowed us with," and that such qualities were incompatible with laity rights.[42]

Bennett acknowledged that she knew the rumor that only childless women and "old maids" supported the proposal; although noting that she considered the remarks about childless women unkind, with self-deprecating humor she refused to defend the unmarrieds. A man who supported laity rights responded by suggesting that perhaps many of the women remained single "because when they look around upon the candidates they say: 'Not for me.'" In a less personal vein, Bennett argued that the restraints on southern women, particularly the barrier that denied Methodist women laity rights, were passing away. "I have not met a man among you," she told the assembled delegates, "who does not say it [the granting of laity rights to women] will eventually come. Then," she continued, "why not let it come now?"[43]

Despite Bennett's pleas, it was not until the next quadrennial meeting of the General Conference in 1918 that laity rights for women won acceptance. The persistence and effectiveness of the women's campaign, buoyed perhaps by the accelerating movement for state and national political suffrage, resulted in an overwhelming vote in favor of the proposal. Arkansas and Texas had admitted women voters to primary elections in 1917 and 1918, respectively, and there were marked gains in state legislative support for women's political suffrage throughout the South. The increasing respectability of participation in organized lobbying for suffrage, evidenced by spectacular growth in local southern auxil-

42. *Journal of the Seventeenth Session of the General Conference,* 214–15; "Proceedings of the General Conference," *Daily Christian Advocate,* XVII (May 21, 1914), 106.
43. W. J. Carpenter, "Proceedings of the General Conference," *Daily Christian Advocate,* XVII (May 21, 1914), 107.

iaries of the National American Woman Suffrage Association between 1910 and 1918, undoubtedly contributed to an atmosphere in which granting laity rights to women in Southern Methodism was far less daring or controversial.[44]

Though the General Conference as a body approved laity rights for women in 1918, the bishops declared the issue a constitutional matter, necessitating ratification by two-thirds of all members of the annual conferences. In taking this action, the bishops maintained that they were not attempting to stymie the legislation, but were merely following precedent established in previous consideration of such lay questions. The bishops had elected to take no formal position on the laity rights proposal in 1918, dropping the opposition they voiced in 1910 and 1914, a decision that probably contributed to the resounding passage of the measure in the General Conference. But the results of the annual-conference voting suggest simply that this was an issue on which Methodists had been thoroughly persuaded; in all forty-four conferences, the measure won majority approval, and an impressive 90 percent of all votes cast favored the granting of laity rights to women.[45]

A major battle had been won, but the women's struggle was hardly completed. As the opponents of laity rights had continually warned, many women soon began to demand a larger role in the life of the church, most dramatically in seeking ordination to the clergy. In June, 1926, the Executive Committee of the Woman's Missionary Council adopted a resolution calling for the appointment of a commission "to study the status of women in the work of our own church at home and abroad in order to discover and define their place of largest usefulness in the work of the Kingdom." The following March the council established the Commission on Woman's Place of Service in the Church. Seven members were appointed, including Mrs. J. C. Handy, the head of the commission.[46]

The commission and its successor, the council's Committee on Research and Study of the Status of Women, became the primary vehicles

44. Shadron, "Out of Our Homes," 127–28.
45. *Journal of the Eighteenth Session of the General Conference*, 61–62.
46. *Report of the Commission on Woman's Place of Service in the Church* (N.p., 1930), 3, 5.

for examining the extent of women's involvement in the Methodist Episcopal Church, South, and for uncovering attitudes toward the participation of women. These groups pointed continually to the underrepresentation of women in the decision-making bodies of the denomination and encouraged women and men to help remove the barriers to greater involvement. They believed that a major barrier was the denial to women of ordination to the clergy. In 1930, on the recommendation of the commission, the council petitioned the General Conference to grant clergy rights to women.[47]

The storm broke over the new call to expand the role of women almost as strongly as it had over the issue of laity rights. However, the arguments on both sides had the ring of familiarity to those acquainted with the earlier struggle. Even more than previously, the issue of woman's biblically prescribed role took center stage. "From the beginning of the Bible to the end," the Reverend J. A. Anderson declared, "there is no word licensing the women to preach. Not one word." The proponents of clergy rights were equally convinced that they were the faithful interpreters of the Scriptures. Mrs. W. J. Piggott warned her listeners at the 1930 General Conference not to be misled by a too-literal reading of the Bible. The true biblical message, she claimed, was Jesus' emphasis on the worth and dignity of each person. She believed that the plea for clergy rights was based "entirely upon what we conceived to be the attitude of Jesus toward women," an attitude that respected the right of each person to fulfill his or her potential. To deny a woman the opportunity of ordination merely because of her gender was to deny her the possibility of her complete development as a person of God.[48]

These now-familiar sentiments were echoed by protagonists on both sides. The split within the denomination over the ordination of women

47. Ibid., 22, 34–38; *Eighteenth Annual Report of the Woman's Missionary Council*, 167–68; *Twenty-second Annual Report of the Woman's Missionary Council*, 157; *Twentieth Annual Report of the Woman's Missionary Council*, 188.
48. "Proceedings of the General Conference," *Daily Christian Advocate*, XXI (May 24, 1930), 124–25. For further evidence of the two opinions, see Mrs. O. E. Hawthorne, "Shall Women Be Ordained to Preach?," Nashville *Christian Advocate*, XCV (March 16, 1934), 348; Mrs. T. I. Charles, "Ordination of Women," Nashville *Christian Advocate*, XCVI (August 16, 1935), 1039–40; S. Stephen McKenney, "Ordination of Women," Nashville *Christian Advocate*, XCVI (September 13, 1935), 1167.

to the clergy was reflected in the action of the 1930 General Conference. After an intense floor debate, the delegates approved, by a vote of 174 to 159, the recommendation of the conference's Committee on Itinerancy "to grant to faithful, called, and prepared women the rights of the clergy on the same basis as they are granted to faithful, called, and prepared men." However, the bishops, who had taken no position on the issue in their address to the conference, again declared the matter a constitutional question. Methodist law required that two-thirds of the conference delegates agree to submit a constitutional question to the annual conferences. Since the proponents of clergy rights could not secure the agreement of such a large majority of the delegates, their cause was, in fact, lost.[49]

Despite the defeat, the women were again encouraged by the support they had received and they were determined to pursue the issue. However, gaining clergy rights proved ultimately more elusive than had laity rights. Although the council petitioned the 1934 General Conference to forbid sexual discrimination in securing any office in the Methodist Episcopal Church, South, the issue failed to receive the support of even a majority of the delegates. Thus, clergy rights for women were farther from reality than they had been four years previously. Because the 1938 General Conference was focusing so much attention on unification, the council decided to forgo attempting to secure clergy rights for women at that meeting.[50]

Although the struggle to open clergy ordination to women in the Methodist Episcopal Church, South, did not succeed, the women vowed to continue to press their cause in the newly formed church. In 1939 their goal was partially realized. The Methodist Church opened clergy ordination to women, as it was already available to women in the Methodist Episcopal and the Methodist Protestant Churches. Although women thus had the opportunity to become ministers in the denomination, they were not granted the right of certain membership in the annual conference, with the concurrent right of appointment. Therefore,

49. *Journal of the Twenty-first Session of the General Conference*, 283, 289–90.
50. *Twenty-first Annual Report of the Woman's Missionary Council*, 60, 159; *Journal of the Twenty-second Session of the General Conference*, 343–44; *Twenty-eighth Annual Report of the Woman's Missionary Council*, 72.

unlike males, female ministers might have no church or church members to pastor. Until 1956, when membership in annual conferences was extended to qualified women, female clergy were in effect still second-class citizens in the church.[51]

The question of a woman's proper role in the church and in society was pivotal in the home mission work of Southern Methodist women throughout its history. From the time of Lucinda Helm's initial efforts to secure an organized work for women in the denomination to the later struggles over organizational autonomy and laity and clergy rights, the women encountered considerable and persistent opposition to their assuming increased activity and authority. Nevertheless, they continued to fight to gain expanded influence. They found support for their cause in their understanding of the Christian message.

God, they were deeply convinced, had called women as well as men to help extend his kingdom in the world. All his followers were to be actively concerned about the spiritual and physical condition of other human beings. Moreover, they believed that God, as manifested especially in the life and words of his son, Jesus, considered women, and in fact all persons, worthy and able beings with potential for divine service. Circumstances changed rapidly during the more than half century of organized home mission work, but the women came eventually to proclaim boldly what they had implied all along—that the gifts and requirements of God knew no limitation by gender. Their emphasis on this conclusion, which involved the women in a number of struggles within their denomination, set them somewhat apart from the many socially concerned Christian men in the late nineteenth and early twentieth centuries who stressed the problems of labor, immigration, or world peace while more or less ignoring women's issues. Yet inevitably, if the history of Southern Methodist women, and other Christian men and women, was to be an account of extending God's kingdom, then it had also to be a story of struggle to achieve full citizenship in that kingdom.

51. *Thirtieth Annual Report of the Woman's Missionary Council*, 33, 180; *Discipline of the Methodist Church* (New York, 1939), 89; *Journal of the 1956 General Conference of the Methodist Church* (New York, 1956), 683–720, 1546; Stevens, *Legacy for the Future*, 41; *Twenty-seventh Annual Report of the Woman's Missionary Council*, 157, 159.

Conclusion

In 1921, Will Alexander wrote to a friend involved in the mission activities of Southern Methodist women that for several years he had been convinced that "the Woman's Missionary Council of the M. E. Church, South, was the most progressive and constructive religious group in the South."[1] That a group of churchwomen should come to receive this accolade from one of the region's leading reformers is surprising. What had these Methodist women done, and what factors had permitted such noteworthy accomplishments?

This study has attempted to portray the scope and diversity of their involvement with social reform causes. The starting point was the home and the family. Their desire to see stable, moral homes among the poor as well as the rich, and among the unchurched as well as the churched, had been a major motivation for beginning home mission work. Their special concern for children had led them to institute orphanages, kindergartens, schools, and settlement projects and inclined them to support unpopular causes such as child labor laws. They recognized that inadequate wages and unsafe working conditions had very real consequences for family stability and well-being and they argued for improved employee working conditions while criticizing the greed of unrestrained capitalism.

Much of their early settlement and city mission work was among immigrant groups that came to various southern cities. These groups brought what the women perceived as the special problems of an alien language and value system, an authoritarian or superstitious religion, and lax morality. Confident of the superiority of their own religion and culture, the women acted quickly at the turn of the century to establish

1. W. W. Alexander to Mrs. Fitzgerald S. Parker, May 4, 1921, in Commission on Interracial Cooperation Papers, Trevor Arnett Library, Atlanta University, Atlanta.

schools and settlement houses to assist and socialize the foreigners who had come to the region.

Their concern for the living conditions and values of native whites and immigrants forced them soon to recognize the dilemma posed by the large black population in the South. Gradually growing in the early years of this century, the work among blacks had by the 1920s and 1930s developed into an extensive enterprise, finding Methodist women at local, conference, and denominational levels supporting the struggle for better schools, jobs, housing, and judicial treatment for blacks. The attitude of condescension that marked their work with immigrants and was evident in the early work among blacks was slowly transformed into a realization that black people, as creatures of God, possessed inherent worth and deserved new respect.

Such a transformation of attitude was integral to their renewed efforts for world peace during the interwar period. Having supported the movement for peace prior to World War I, they eventually came to rethink their own halting acceptance of that conflict and to conclude that the dreadful consequences of war forbade any optimism about its benefits.

The women's work on behalf of social reform came also to include the reform of their own condition in their denomination. They struggled, with mixed results, to maintain the autonomy of their mission organization and to secure equal rights and privileges as lay members and as clergy. In these struggles, as in their other work, we can begin to perceive the factors that permitted them to attempt and accomplish such extensive social change.

No single explanation of why these Methodist women became caught up in a whirlwind of activity will suffice. The evidence points to a host of factors that interacted to influence their involvement. As Methodists, these women were part of a religious tradition that emphasized the importance of ethical activity and the possibility of human improvement. Nineteenth-century Methodists, though usually northerners, had expanded these perfectionist themes and sought numerous societal reforms on the basis of these convictions; the women of Southern Methodism were beneficiaries of their legacy. This tradition was rooted fundamentally in a theology that stressed God's concern and love for all people and that emphasized the possibility of each person's free response. The women assimilated these central Methodist beliefs and reinterpreted them in their own day to undergird a strong conviction of the worth and dignity of the individual. Methodism also provided the women a connectional system of government, one carefully organized from the local to the denominational level. Such a structure made it easier for Methodist women to establish a denomination-wide organization than it was for their Baptist or Presbyterian counterparts, whose local and regional bodies had more authority. That the home mission organization was composed of women who elected to join, rather than all the women of the denomination, may have limited its membership, but this also gave the group additional coherence and probably permitted it to assume a more radical posture.

The home mission workers also benefited from the expanding opportunities available to women in society, even in the South, during the period of their involvement. As the most accessible institution outside the home, the church quite naturally proved fertile ground for women seeking an active social role. Southern Methodist women were prepared to take advantage of the considerable autonomy the males in their denomination permitted their initial mission work; of particular importance was the authority granted by the denomination to the women to raise and spend their own money. This independence, even if most plausibly explained as the result of male indifference to the women's activities, worked to the advantage of the home mission movement by giving free rein to the women's organizational talents and their ideas.

Despite the frequent benefits of seeming indifference from some quarters, the history of the work described herein demonstrates that the women often encountered substantial opposition from men and some women in the denomination and certainly from many outside the church. Significantly, however, most of the women who assumed positions of leadership were not opposed by their own husbands and families. Some of the leaders, such as Belle Bennett and Lucinda Helm, were unmarried and others, such as Bertha Newell and Tochie MacDonell, had husbands who served as Methodist ministers and were usually more sympathetic to the women's involvement with church work. Still others, like Dorothy Tilly and Bessie Alford, had husbands who, though not ministers, supported the work they undertook. The emotional distance of the opposition seems to have made controversial forms of service feasible. When there was opposition from family to some mission project, such as Mary DeBardeleben's work among blacks, there was a sizable community of Methodist women ready to offer support to counter that opposition. The availability of such support does not minimize the personal courage necessary for some of the women's actions on behalf of the home mission cause, yet it perhaps explains to some degree why projects that risked the disapproval of the larger community could be undertaken.

As American Protestants, the women were also significantly affected by the widening interest in socially concerned Christianity during much of the period of their work. They read and studied the writings of many Social Gospel leaders, invited some of them to their meetings, and were demonstrably influenced by a variety of their ideas. In conformity with other proponents of a social gospel, the women understood their mission work primarily in terms of extending God's kingdom on earth. God, they believed, had commanded his followers to minister to the whole person, including physical and social as well as spiritual needs. For the Christian worker, there was no unbridgeable chasm between the secular world and the sacred world; Christianity should concern itself with the salvation of the entire person and the whole earth.

While working to extend God's kingdom, the women also articulated and acted according to additional ideas shared with other Christians working for social reform. The most fundamental was the conviction that all people are valuable creations of God, deemed worthy and capable by him and able in their freedom to respond to his love and live redeemed lives. The women accepted the corollary that Christians, as God's followers, ought also to respect the inherent value and potential in other persons. This viewpoint buttressed the women's belief that both individual lives and the course of history could be improved. This persistent optimism undergirded all the women's activities; progress was seen as possible if people work for it. Yet progress remained contingent upon a reformed environment. The women's emphasis on human freedom and effort did not mitigate the importance they attached to sur-

148 / The Social Gospel in the South

roundings. A person's body, mind, and soul could be crippled by the conditions amid which he lived. Therefore, it was imperative that the Christian reform those conditions.

Thus various elements—religious ideas, denominational structures, societal influences, and personal relationships—combined to aid the women in carrying out this progressive and constructive work. They would, no doubt, acknowledge that the history of their activities is a mixture of condescension and mutual acceptance, of timidity and courage. Their story is one of expanding numbers and finances, of changing attitudes, and of an increasingly diversified and growing range of interests. In spite of many variations, their more than half century of home mission work reflects a consistent picture of an active social Christianity. Their involvement with social problems does not completely overturn the widely held impression that southern religion has focused primarily on individual salvation and personal morality. Nevertheless, it does indicate that social Christianity has played a perhaps surprisingly significant role in the religious history of the South, and also makes clear that we must consider more carefully the work and ideas of frequently overlooked groups if we are to create an accurate picture of religious trends in the South.

Bibliography

Primary Sources

Annual Report of the Board of Church Extension of the Methodist Episcopal Church, South. Vols. IV–VIII. Nashville: Publishing House of the Methodist Episcopal Church, South, 1886–90.

Annual Report of the Woman's Home Mission Society of the Methodist Episcopal Church, South. [Title varies.] Vols. VI–VIII, X–XXIV. Nashville: Publishing House of the MEC, S, 1892–94, 1896–1910.

Annual Report of the Woman's Missionary Council of the Methodist Episcopal Church, South. Vols. I–XXX. Nashville: Publishing House of the MEC, S, 1911–40.

Daily Christian Advocate. Vols. XI, XV–XIX [1886, 1902–1918].

Journal of the General Conference of the Methodist Episcopal Church, South. Vols. X–XXIII. Nashville: Publishing House of the MEC, S, 1886–1938.

Missionary Voice, 1911–32.

Our Homes, 1892–1910.

World Outlook, 1932–40.

Articles by or About Southern Methodist Women

Allen, H. T. "Laity Rights for Women." Nashville *Christian Advocate*, LXXV (May 1, 1914), 555–56.

Barber, Mrs. R. W. "Home Missions." *Southern Christian Advocate*, LXXI (April 4, 1907), 6.

Barcus, John M. "Woman's Rights in the Church." Nashville *Christian Advocate*, LXXI (April 1, 1910), 391.

Briggs, A. C. "The Ordination of Women." Nashville *Christian Advocate*, XCV (May 4, 1934), 558–59.

Charles, Mrs. T. I. "Ordination of Women." Nashville *Christian Advocate*, XCVI (August 16, 1935), 1039–40.

———. "Ordination of Women." Nashville *Christian Advocate*, XCVI (September 6, 1935), 1136.

Court, Mrs. William. "Social Service Lines of Home Mission Work." *Methodist Quarterly Review*, LXII (October, 1913), 764–67.

Courtenay, Austen Matlack. "Deaconesses: A Brief Study of the Diaconate of Women." *Methodist Quarterly Review*, LII (January, 1903), 77–87.

"Deaconesses." Nashville *Christian Advocate*, LXVI (June 29, 1905), 3.

Downs, Francis A. "The Greatest Woman in Southern Methodism." *Methodist Quarterly Review*, LXIV (April, 1915), 255–66.

Evans, W. F. "Lay Women or Not?" Nashville *Christian Advocate*, LXXI (April 29, 1910), 531.

Goodman, Mrs. W. F. "Our Broadened Opportunities." *North Carolina Christian Advocate*, LVI (December 8, 1910), 11.

Hammond, Mrs. John D. [Lily H.] "The Growth of Democracy in the South." *Methodist Quarterly Review*, LIV (January, 1905), 28–38.

––––––. "Human Races and the Race of Man." *Methodist Quarterly Review*, LXXIII (October, 1924), 623–33.

––––––. "Ignorance and the Eleven Million." *Nation's Business*, VIII (December, 1920), 38–40.

––––––. "Light on Negro Delinquency." Nashville *Christian Advocate*, LXXV (October 16, 1914), 26–27.

––––––. "Negro Condemnation of Negro Criminals." Nashville *Christian Advocate*, LXXX (August 22, 1919), 1080.

––––––. "New Light on Social Problems." *Methodist Review*, XLII (January–February, 1896), 376–83.

––––––. "Present-Day Philanthropy." *Methodist Quarterly Review*, LIII (January, 1904), 25–35.

––––––. "Some Southern Factory Problems." *Methodist Review*, LI (May–June, 1902), 349–59.

––––––. "A Southern View of the Negro." *Outlook*, LXXIII (March 14, 1903), 619–23.

––––––. "Wasted Power." Nashville *Christian Advocate*, LXXV (August 7, 1914), 10–11.

––––––. "Women Novelists and Marriage." *Methodist Quarterly Review*, LII (April, 1903), 319–23.

Haskin, [Sara] Estelle. "Women as Lay Members—What Will It Profit?" Baltimore and Richmond *Christian Advocate*, IX (February 24, 1910), 2.

Hawthorne, Mrs. O. E. "Shall Women Be Ordained to Preach?" Nashville *Christian Advocate*, XCV (March 16, 1934), 348.

Helm, Mary. "The Memorial of the Woman's Board." Nashville *Christian Advocate*, LXXI (April 15, 1910), 469.

––––––. "The Problem of Domestic Service." *Methodist Quarterly Review*, LXI (October, 1912), 703–719.

––––––. "Shall Right Yield to Opposition?" Baltimore and Richmond *Christian Advocate*, IX (March 17, 1910), 11.

Hendrix, Eugene Russell. "The Sisters of Jesus." *Methodist Quarterly Review*, LII (July, 1903), 467–84.

Herbert, Mrs. E. S. "Temperance and Home Mission Work." *Southern Christian Advocate*, LXVII (April 14, 1904), 14.

MacDonell, Mrs. R. W. [Tochie.] "Why Women Ask the Rights of the Laity." Nashville *Christian Advocate*, LXX (November 19, 1909), 24–25.

MacDonell, Mrs. R. W. [Tochie], and Mrs. J. B. Cobb. "The Board of Missions and the Woman's Work of the Church." *North Carolina Christian Advocate*, LV (August 4, 1910), 6.

McKenney, S. Stephen. "Ordination of Women." Nashville *Christian Advocate*, XCVI (September 13, 1935), 1167.

Meade, Emily Fogg. "Italian Immigration into the South." *South Atlantic Quarterly*, IV (July, 1905), 217–23.

Moore, Mary N. "Shall Our Methodism Accord Women the Privileges of the Laity?" *Methodist Quarterly Review*, LXII (October, 1913), 733–38.

Perry, Mrs. J. W. "The Memorial of the Woman's Home Mission Board." Nashville *Christian Advocate*, LXXI (April 15, 1910), 475–76.

————. "Why the Women of the Church Do Not Want the Rights of the Laity." *Southern Christian Advocate*, LXXIII (February 24, 1910), 2–3.

Reaves, E. C. "Equal Rights and Privileges with the Laity." Nashville *Christian Advocate*, LXXI (April 15, 1910), 470.

"Social Settlements and the Church." Nashville *Christian Advocate*, LXIV (June 18, 1903), 1.

Taylor, Graham. "The Southern Social Awakening." *Survey*, XXVIII (September 14, 1912), 744–45.

Townsend, Mrs. F. L. "Why I Am Opposed to Woman's Suffrage." *Methodist Quarterly Review*, LXII (January, 1913), 98–107.

Trawick, A. M., Jr. "Woman's Representation." Nashville *Christian Advocate*, LXXI (February 25, 1910), 8–11.

Turpin, Maud M. "Women on the Boards: A Parable." Nashville *Christian Advocate*, XCVII (February 7, 1936), 174–75.

"Women's Representation." Nashville *Christian Advocate*, LXXI (April 1, 1910), 407–408.

Books by or About Southern Methodist Women

Alexander, Arabel W. *Life and Work of Lucinda B. Helm*. Nashville: Publishing House of the MEC, S, 1904.

Ames, Jessie Daniel, and Bertha Payne Newell. *Repairers of the Breach: A Story of Interracial Cooperation Between Southern Women, 1935–1940*. Atlanta: Commission on Interracial Cooperation, 1940.

Brown, O. E., and Anna Muse Brown. *Life and Letters of Laura Askew Haygood*. Nashville: Smith and Lamar, 1904.

Brown, R. K. *Life of Mrs. M. L. Kelley*. N.p.: By the Author, 1889.

Butler, Sarah F. *History of the Woman's Foreign Missionary Society, M. E. Church, South*. Nashville: Smith, 1912.

————. *Mrs. D. H. M'Gavock: Life-Sketch and Thoughts*. Nashville: Publishing House of the MEC, S, n.d.

Dunn, Mary Noreen. *Women and Home Missions*. Nashville: Cokesbury Press, 1936.

Gibson, Maria Layng. *Memories of Scarritt*. Edited and completed by Sara Estelle Haskin. Nashville: Cokesbury Press, 1928.

Goddard, O. E., and Mrs. R. W. [Tochie] MacDonell. *Making America Safe: A Study of the Home Missions of the Methodist Episcopal Church, South*. Nashville: Centenary Commission, MEC, S, n.d.

Hammond, Lily H. *In Black and White: An Interpretation of Southern Life.* New York: Fleming H. Revell, 1914.
———. *In the Vanguard of a Race.* New York: Council of Women for Home Missions and Missionary Education Movement of the United States and Canada, 1922.
———. *Southern Women and Racial Adjustment.* Lynchburg, Va.: J. P. Bell, 1917.
Harris, Mrs. W. R. *Fifty Years of Missionary Achievement, 1890–1940: Historical Sketch of Woman's Missionary Society, Western North Carolina Conference.* N.p.: Woman's Missionary Society, Western North Carolina Conference, 1940.
Haskin, Sara Estelle. *The Handicapped Winners.* 2nd ed. Nashville: Publishing House of the MEC, S, 1925.
———. *Women and Missions in the Methodist Episcopal Church, South.* Nashville: Publishing House of the MEC, S, 1925.
Haskin, Sara Estelle [assisted by Rebecca Caudill]. *The Upward Climb: A Course in Negro Achievement.* New York: Council of Women for Home Missions, 1927.
Helm, Mary. *From Darkness to Light: The Story of Negro Progress.* 2nd ed. New York: Fleming H. Revell, 1909.
———. *The Upward Path: The Evolution of a Race.* Cincinnati: Jennings and Graham, 1909.
Herbert, Walter J. *Fifty Wonderful Years, 1878–1928: Story of Missionary Work by Methodist Women in South Carolina, Methodist Episcopal Church, South.* N.p.: Jubilee Committees of the Two South Carolina Conferences, 1928.
Howell, Mabel Katherine. *Women and the Kingdom: Fifty Years of Kingdom Building by the Women of the Methodist Episcopal Church, South, 1878–1928.* Nashville: Cokesbury Press, 1928.
Hoyland, John S. *The Teaching of Jesus on Human Relations.* Adapted by Mary DeBardeleben. New York: Abingdon-Cokesbury Press, n.d.
MacDonell, Mrs. R. W. [Tochie.] *Belle Harris Bennett: Her Life Work.* Nashville: Woman's Section of the Board of Missions, MEC, S, 1928.
Olmstead, Emily K. *Intimate Glimpses of Miss Belle Bennett.* Nashville: MEC, S, 1923.
Report of the Commission on Woman's Place of Service in the Church. N.p.: Woman's Missionary Council, MEC, S, 1930.
Tatum, Noreen Dunn. *A Crown of Service: A Story of Woman's Work in the Methodist Episcopal Church, South, from 1878–1940.* Nashville: Parthenon Press, 1960.
Williams, Cora G. *The Morning-Glory: Life and Work of Miss Mae McKenzie, Deaconess.* Nashville: Publishing House of the MEC, S, 1910.

Interviews and Manuscript Collections

Ames, Jessie Daniel. Collected Papers. Southern Historical Collection, University of North Carolina, Chapel Hill.

———. Collection. Manuscript Department, Duke University, Durham, N.C.
Association of Southern Women for the Prevention of Lynching Papers. Trevor Arnett Library, Atlanta University, Atlanta.
Clark, James Osgood Andrew. Papers. Woodruff Library, Emory University, Atlanta.
Commission on Interracial Cooperation Papers. Trevor Arnett Library, Atlanta University, Atlanta.
Duke Memorial Church: Woman's Missionary Society Papers. Manuscript Department, Duke University, Durham, N.C.
Everett, Lillie Moore. Collection. Manuscript Department, Duke University, Durham, N.C.
Heartsill, Fannie A. Papers. Barker Texas History Center, University of Texas at Austin.
North Georgia Conference Records, Woman's Missionary Society. Pitts Theological Library, Emory University, Atlanta.
Stevens, Thelma. Interview, February 14, 1972. Southern Oral History Program, Southern Historical Collection, University of North Carolina, Chapel Hill.
Tilly, Dorothy Rogers. Papers. Woodruff Library, Emory University, Atlanta.
Young, Louise. Interview, February 14, 1972. Southern Oral History Program, Southern Historical Collection, University of North Carolina, Chapel Hill.

Secondary Sources

Articles

Bailey, Kenneth K. "Southern White Protestantism at the Turn of the Century." *American Historical Review*, LXVIII (1963), 618–35.
Bassett, John Spenser. "Stirring Up the Fires of Race Antipathy." *South Atlantic Quarterly*, II (October, 1903), 297–305.
Berthoff, Rowland T. "Southern Attitudes Toward Immigration, 1865–1914." *Journal of Southern History*, XVII (1951), 328–60.
Chatfield, E. Charles. "The Southern Sociological Congress: Organization of Uplift." *Tennessee Historical Quarterly*, XIX (1960), 328–47.
———. "The Southern Sociological Congress: Rationale of Uplift." *Tennessee Historical Quarterly*, XX (1961), 51–64.
Doherty, Herbert J., Jr. "Voices of Protest from the New South, 1875–1910." *Mississippi Valley Historical Review*, XLII (1955), 45–66.
Eighmy, John L. "Religious Liberalism in the South During the Progressive Era." *Church History*, XXXVII (September, 1969), 359–72.
Flint, Wayne. "Dissent in Zion: Alabama Baptists and Social Issues, 1900–1914." *Journal of Southern History*, XXXV (1969), 523–42.
Hutchison, William R. "Cultural Strains and Protestant Liberalism." *American Historical Review*, LXXVI (1971), 386–411.

Luker, Ralph E. "The Social Gospel and the Failure of Racial Reform, 1877–1898." *Church History*, XLVI (March, 1977), 80–99.
Manschreck, Clyde L. "Religion in the South: Problem and Promise." In *The South in Perspective*, edited by Francis B. Simkins. Farmerville, Va.: Longwood College, 1959.
Miller, Robert M. "Southern White Protestantism and the Negro, 1865–1965." In *The Negro in the South Since 1865: Selected Essays in American Negro History*, edited by Charles E. Wynes. University, Ala.: University of Alabama Press, 1965.
Poteat, Edwin M., Jr. "Religion in the South." In *Culture in the South*, edited by W. T. Couch. Chapel Hill: University of North Carolina Press, 1934.
Schlesinger, Arthur M. "A Critical Period in American Religion, 1875–1900." *Massachusetts Historical Society Proceedings*, LXIV (1932), 523–47.
Scott, Anne F. "After Suffrage: Southern Women in the Twenties." *Journal of Southern History*, XXX (1964), 298–318.
———. "The 'New Woman' in the New South." *South Atlantic Quarterly*, LXI (1962), 473–83.
———. "A Progressive Wind from the South, 1906–1913." *Journal of Southern History*, XXIX (1963), 53–70.
Simkins, Francis B. "The Newer Religiousness." *Georgia Review*, IV (Summer, 1950), 75–84.
Smith, Timothy L. "The Holiness Crusade." In *The History of American Methodism*, II, edited by Emory S. Bucke. New York: Abingdon Press, 1964.
Swing, David. "The Failure of the Southern Pulpit." *North American Review*, CXXX (April, 1880), 356–69.
Tindall, George. "The Central Theme Revisited." In *The Southerner as American*, edited by Charles G. Sellers. Chapel Hill: University of North Carolina Press, 1960.
Warnock, Henry Y. "Andrew Sledd, Southern Methodist, and the Negro: A Case History." *Journal of Southern History*, XXXI (1965), 251–71.

Books

Abell, Aaron I. *The Urban Impact on American Protestantism, 1865–1900.* Cambridge: Harvard University Press, 1943.
Abrams, Ray H. *Preachers Present Arms.* New York: Round Table Press, 1933.
Alexander, Gross. *History of the Methodist Church, South.* New York: Christian Literature Co., 1894.
Anthony, Susan B., et al. *History of Woman Suffrage.* 6 vols. Rochester: n.p., 1887–1922.
Bailey, Kenneth K. *Southern White Protestantism in the Twentieth Century.* New York: Harper and Row, 1964.
Baker, Paul E. *Negro-White Adjustment: An Investigation and Analysis of Methods in the Interracial Movement in the United States.* New York: Association Press, 1934.

Barclay, Wade Crawford. *The Methodist Episcopal Church: Widening Horizons, 1845–1895.* New York: Board of Missions, Methodist Church, 1957.

Beaver, R. Pierce. *All Loves Excelling: American Protestant Women in World Mission.* Grand Rapids: William B. Eerdmans, 1968.

Bell, W. A. *Missions and Co-operation of the Methodist Episcopal Church, South with the Colored Methodist Episcopal Church: A Study.* N.p.: For the Commission on Co-operation and Counsel, MEC, S, and the Colored Methodist Episcopal Church, 1932–33.

Blanshard, Paul. *Labor in the Southern Cotton Mills.* New York: New Republic, 1927.

Blum, John M., et al. *The National Experience.* 2nd ed. New York: Harcourt, Brace and World, 1968.

Bode, Frederick A. *Protestantism and the New South: North Carolina Baptists and Methodists in Political Crisis, 1894–1903.* Charlottesville: University Press of Virginia, 1975.

Boeckel, Florence B. *The Turn Toward Peace.* New York: Friendship Press, 1930.

Bremer, Robert H., ed. *Children and Youth in America.* Vol. II, *1866–1932.* Cambridge: Harvard University Press, 1971.

Brunner, Edmund deS. *Church Life in the Rural South.* New York: George H. Doran, 1923.

Calkins, Gladys Gilkey. *Follow Those Women: Church Women in the Ecumenical Movement.* New York: National Council of Churches, 1961.

Cannon, James, III. *History of Southern Methodist Missions.* Nashville: Cokesbury Press, 1926.

Carter, Paul Allen. *The Decline and Rise of the Social Gospel.* Ithaca, N.Y.: Cornell University Press, 1956.

———. *The Idea of Progress in American Protestant Thought, 1930–1960.* Philadelphia: Fortress Press, 1969.

Cash, Wilbur J. *The Mind of the South.* New York: Vintage Books, 1941.

Clark, Elmer T. *The Church and the World Parish.* Nashville: Board of Missions, MEC, S, 1929.

Clark, Thomas D., and Albert D. Kirwan. *The South Since Appomattox: A Century of Regional Change.* New York: Oxford University Press, 1967.

Clebsch, William A. *From Sacred to Profane America: The Role of Religion in American History.* New York: Harper and Row, 1968.

Croly, Mrs. J. C. *The History of the Woman's Club Movement in America.* New York: H. G. Allen, 1898.

Culver, Dwight W. *Negro Segregation in the Methodist Church.* New Haven: Yale University Press, 1953.

Dabney, Virginius. *Liberalism in the South.* Chapel Hill: University of North Carolina Press, 1932.

Daniels, Jonathan. *A Southerner Discovers the South.* New York: Macmillan, 1938.

Davie, Maurice R. *World Immigration: With Special Reference to the United States.* New York: Macmillan, 1936.

Discipline of the Methodist Church. New York: Methodist Publishing House, 1939.

Douglass, H. Paul. *Christian Reconstruction in the South.* Boston: Pilgrim Press, 1909.

DuBose, Horace M. *A History of Methodism.* Nashville: Publishing House of the MEC, S, 1916.

Dykeman, Wilma. *Prophet of Plenty: The First Ninety Years of W. D. Weatherford.* Knoxville: University of Tennessee Press, 1966.

Dykeman, Wilma, and James Stokely. *Seeds of Southern Change: The Life of Will Alexander.* Chicago: University of Chicago Press, 1962.

Eighmy, John L. *Churches in Cultural Captivity: A History of the Social Attitudes of Southern Baptists.* Knoxville: University of Tennessee Press, 1972.

Ezell, John S. *The South Since 1865.* New York: Macmillan, 1963.

Farish, Hunter Dickinson. *The Circuit Rider Dismounts: A Social History of Southern Methodism, 1865–1900.* Richmond: Dietz Press, 1938.

Flexner, Eleanor. *Century of Struggle: The Woman's Rights Movement in the United States.* Cambridge: Harvard University Press, 1959.

Frazier, E. Franklin. *The Negro Church in America.* [Published as one volume with C. Eric Lincoln, *The Black Church Since Frazier.*] New York: Schocken Books, 1974.

Gaston, Paul M. *The New South Creed.* New York: Alfred A. Knopf, 1970.

Gaustad, Edwin S. *Historical Atlas of Religion in America.* New York: Harper and Row, 1962.

Gladden, Washington. *Applied Christianity.* Boston: Houghton Mifflin, 1899.

Glasgow, Ellen. *The Woman Within.* New York: Harcourt, Brace, 1954.

Goldman, Eric F. *Rendezvous with Destiny.* New York: Alfred A. Knopf, 1952.

Gordon, Anna A. *The Life of Frances Willard.* Evanston: Lakeside Press, 1912.

Gossett, Thomas F. *Race: The History of an Idea in America.* Dallas: Southern Methodist University Press, 1963.

Grob, Gerald N. *Mental Institutions in America: Social Policy to 1875.* New York: Free Press, 1973.

Hahn, Emily. *Once Upon a Pedestal.* New York: Thomas Y. Crowell, 1974.

Hall, Jacquelyn Dowd. *Revolt Against Chivalry: Jessie Daniel Ames and the Women's Campaign Against Lynching.* New York: Columbia University Press, 1979.

Handy, Robert T., ed. *The Social Gospel in America, 1870–1920.* New York: Oxford University Press, 1966.

Hesseltine, W. B., and David L. Smiley. *The South in American History.* 2nd ed. Englewood Cliffs, N.J.: Prentice-Hall, 1960.

Higham, John. *Send These to Me: Jews and Other Immigrants in Urban America.* New York: Atheneum, 1975.

Hill, Samuel S., Jr. *Southern Churches in Crisis.* New York: Holt, Rinehart and Winston, 1967.

————, ed. *Religion and the Solid South.* Nashville: Abingdon Press, 1972.

Hopkins, Charles H. *The Rise of the Social Gospel in American Protestantism, 1865–1915.* New Haven: Yale University Press, 1940.

Hutchison, William. *The Modernist Impulse in America.* Cambridge: Harvard University Press, 1976.

I'll Take My Stand: The South and the Agrarian Tradition. New York: Harper and Brothers, 1930.

Johnson, Charles S. *A Preface to Racial Understanding.* New York: Friendship Press, 1936.

Journal of the 1956 General Conference of the Methodist Church. New York: Methodist Publishing House, 1956.

Kraditor, Aileen. *The Ideas of the Woman Suffrage Movement, 1890–1920.* New York: Columbia University Press, 1965.

Kutler, Stanley I., and Stanley N. Katz, eds. *Reviews in American History.* Vols. I–VI. Westport, Conn.: Redgrave Information Resources Corp., 1973–78.

Lasch, Christopher. *Haven in a Heartless World: The Family Besieged.* New York: Basic Books, 1977.

Loveland, Anne C. *Southern Evangelicals and the Social Order, 1800–1860.* Baton Rouge: Louisiana State University Press, 1980.

Lumpkin, Katharine Du Pre. *The Making of a Southerner.* New York: Alfred A. Knopf, 1947.

McCulloch, James E., ed. *Battling for Social Betterment.* Nashville: Southern Sociological Congress, 1914.

———, ed. *The Call of the New South.* Nashville: Southern Sociological Congress, 1912.

———, ed. *The New Chivalry—Health.* Nashville: Southern Sociological Congress, 1915.

———, ed. *The South Mobilizing for Social Service.* Nashville: Southern Sociological Congress, 1913.

McGill, Ralph E. *The South and the Southerner.* Boston: Little, Brown, 1963.

McKinney, John C., and Edgar T. Thompson, eds. *The South in Continuity and Change.* Durham, N.C.: Duke University Press, 1965.

McTyeire, Holland N. *A History of Methodism.* Nashville: Publishing House of the MEC, S, 1919.

Mann, Harold W. *Atticus Greene Haygood: Methodist Bishop, Editor, and Educator.* Athens: University of Georgia Press, 1965.

Masters, Victor I. *Country Church in the South.* Atlanta: Home Mission Board, Southern Baptist Convention, 1917.

Mathews, Donald G. *Religion in the Old South.* Chicago: University of Chicago Press, 1977.

May, Henry F. *Protestant Churches and Industrial America.* New York: Harper and Brothers, 1949.

Meeker, Ruth Esther. *Six Decades of Service, 1880–1940: A History of the Woman's Home Missionary Society of the Methodist Episcopal Church.* Cincinnati: Steinhauser, 1969.

Mencken, H. L. *Prejudices: A Selection.* Selected and introduced by James T. Farrell. New York: Vintage Books, 1958.

Merrick, Caroline E. *Old Time in Dixie Land.* New York: Grafton Press, 1901.

Meyer, Donald. *The Protestant Search for Political Realism.* Berkeley: University of California Press, 1960.

Miller, Robert M. *American Protestantism and Social Issues, 1919–1939*. Chapel Hill: University of North Carolina Press, 1958.

Mims, Edwin. *The Advancing South*. Garden City, N.Y.: Doubleday, Page, 1927.

Mitchell, Broadus, and George S. Mitchell. *The Industrial Revolution in the South*. Baltimore: Johns Hopkins Press, 1930.

Myrdal, Gunnar. *An American Dilemma: The Negro Problem and Modern Democracy*. 2 vols. New York and London: Harper and Brothers, 1944.

Negro Population in the United States, 1790–1915. New York: Arno Press and the New York Times, 1968.

Odum, Howard W. *Southern Regions of the United States*. Chapel Hill: University of North Carolina Press, 1936.

O'Neill, William L. *Everyone Was Brave: The Rise and Fall of Feminism in America*. Chicago: Quadrangle Books, 1969.

Outler, Albert C. *Theology in the Wesleyan Spirit*. Nashville: Tidings, 1975.

————, ed. *John Wesley: A Representative Collection of His Writings*. New York: Oxford University Press, 1964.

Pivar, David J. *Purity Crusade: Sexual Morality and Social Control, 1868–1900*. Westport, Conn.: Greenwood Press, 1973.

Pope, Liston. *Millhands and Preachers: A Study of Gastonia*. New Haven: Yale University Press, 1942.

Rauschenbusch, Walter. *Christianity and the Social Crisis*. New York: Macmillan, 1907.

————. *Christianizing the Social Order*. New York: Macmillan, 1912.

————. *A Theology for the Social Gospel*. New York: Macmillan, 1917.

Rawlings, E. H. *Yet Another Day in Methodist Missions*. Nashville: Publishing House of the MEC, S, 1927.

Reimers, David M. *White Protestantism and the Negro*. New York: Oxford University Press, 1965.

Riegel, Robert E. *American Feminists*. Lawrence: University Press of Kansas, 1963.

Rosenberg, Carroll Smith. *Religion and the Rise of the American City: The New York City Mission Movement, 1812–1870*. Ithaca, N.Y.: Cornell University Press, 1871.

Rubin, Louis D., Jr., and James J. Kilpatrick, eds. *The Lasting South: Fourteen Southerners Look at Their Home*. Chicago: Henry Regnery, 1957.

Scott, Anne F. *The Southern Lady: From Pedestal to Politics, 1830–1930*. Chicago: University of Chicago Press, 1970.

Second Annual Report of the Woman's Division of Christian Service of the Board of Missions and Church Extension of the Methodist Church. New York: Methodist Church, 1942.

Simkins, Francis B. *The Everlasting South*. Baton Rouge: Louisiana State University Press, 1963.

————. *A History of the South*. 3rd ed. New York: Alfred A. Knopf, 1963.

Sinclair, Andrew. *The Better Half: The Emancipation of the American Woman*. New York: Harper and Row, 1965.

Sklar, Robert. *Movie-Made America: A Social History of American Movies.* New York: Random House, 1975.

Sledge, Robert Watson. *Hands on the Ark: The Struggle for Change in the Methodist Episcopal Church, South, 1914–1939.* Lake Junaluska, N.C.: Commission on Archives and History, United Methodist Church, 1975.

Smith, H. Shelton. *In His Image, But . . . .: Racism in Southern Religion, 1780–1910.* Durham, N.C.: Duke University Press, 1972.

Smith, Timothy L. *Revivalism and Social Reform in Mid-Nineteenth-Century America.* New York: Abingdon Press, 1957.

Stevens, Thelma. *Legacy for the Future: The History of Christian Social Relations in the Woman's Division of Christian Service, 1940–1968.* Cincinnati: Women's Division, Board of Global Ministries, United Methodist Church, 1978.

Strong, Josiah. *The New Era.* New York: Baker and Taylor, 1893.

————. *Our Country.* New York: Baker and Taylor, 1891.

Thompson, Ernest Trice. *Presbyterians in the South.* Vol. III, *1890–1972.* Richmond: John Knox Press, 1973.

Tindall, George. *The Emergence of the New South, 1913–1945.* Baton Rouge: Louisiana State University Press, 1967.

Vandiver, Frank E., ed. *The Idea of the South: Pursuit of a Central Theme.* Chicago: University of Chicago Press, 1964.

Watson, Richard L., ed. *Bishop Cannon's Own Story: Life as I Have Seen It.* Durham, N.C.: Duke University Press, 1955.

Weatherford, Willis D. *American Churches and the Negro: An Historical Study from the Early Slave Days to the Present.* Boston: Christopher Publishing House, 1957.

————. *Interracial Cooperation: A Study of the Various Agencies Working in the Field of Social Welfare.* N.p.: Interracial Committee, War Work Council, YMCA, n.d.

Weatherford, Willis D., and Charles S. Johnson. *Race Relations: Adjustment of Whites and Negroes in the United States.* Boston: D. C. Heath, 1934.

Welter, Barbara. *Dimity Convictions: The American Woman in the Nineteenth Century.* Athens: Ohio University Press, 1976.

White, Donald C., Jr., and Charles Howard Hopkins. *The Social Gospel: Religion and Reform in Changing America.* Philadelphia: Temple University Press, 1976.

White, Walter F. *Rope and Faggott: A Biography of Judge Lynch.* New York: Alfred A. Knopf, 1929.

Willard, Frances E. *Glimpses of Fifty Years.* Chicago: Woman's Temperance Publication Assoc., 1889.

Woodward, C. Vann. *The Burden of Southern History.* 2nd ed. Baton Rouge: Louisiana State University Press, 1968.

————. *Origins of the New South, 1877–1913.* 2nd ed. Baton Rouge: Louisiana State University Press, 1971.

————. *The Strange Career of Jim Crow.* 3rd rev. ed. New York: Oxford University Press, 1974.

Theses and Dissertations

Autry, John D. A. "History of the Woman's Missionary Council, Methodist Episcopal Church, South, 1910–1940." B.D. thesis, Duke University, 1940.

Culley, John J. "Muted Trumpets: Four Efforts to Better Southern Race Relations, 1900–1919." Ph.D. dissertation, University of Virginia, 1967.

Fair, Harold Lloyd. "Southern Methodists on Education and Race, 1900–1920." Ph.D. dissertation, Vanderbilt University, 1971.

Fish, John D. "Southern Methodism in the Progressive Era: A Social History." Ph.D. dissertation, University of Georgia, 1969.

Mitchell, Frank J. "The Virginia Methodist Conference and Social Issues in the Twentieth Century." Ph.D. dissertation, Duke University, 1962.

Shadron, Virginia A. "Out of Our Homes: The Woman's Rights Movement in the Methodist Episcopal Church, South, 1890–1918." M.A. thesis, Emory University, 1976.

Spain, Rufus B. "Attitudes and Reactions of Southern Baptists to Certain Problems of Society, 1865–1900." Ph.D. dissertation, Vanderbilt University, 1961.

Warnock, Henry Y. "Moderate Racial Thought and Attitudes of Southern Baptists and Methodists, 1900–1921." Ph.D. dissertation, Northwestern University, 1963.

Index

Abell, Aaron, 1
Abrams, Ray H., 74n
Ada (Okla.), 40
Addams, Jane, 61
Alcohol. *See* Temperance movement
Alexander, Arabel, 37
Alexander, Will, 86, 88, 89, 90, 91, 95,
  101, 144
Alford, Bessie, 97, 147
Allen, Emily, 73
Allen, Reverend H. T., 132
Ames, Jessie Daniel, 91, 95, 96, 97, 98,
  113
Anderson, Reverend J. A., 141
Anne Browder Cunningham Mission
  Home and Training School (Dallas),
  25
Asheville (N.C.), 126
Association of Southern Women for the
  Prevention of Lynching (ASWPL), 95,
  97, 98
Atlanta: meetings in, 64, 95; mission
  work in, 9, 13, 61; mentioned, 87n, 88
Augusta: mission work in, 86, 113; men-
  tioned, 84

Baltimore, 9
Barcus, J. M., 133, 137
Bennett, Belle: biography of, 26, 146; and
  child labor, 42; and home mission
  work, 25, 26, 61–62, 65, 84, 93n; and
  political action, 41, 57–58; and race
  problems, 94, 100, 105n; and World
  War I, 73–74, 75, 77–78; on moral
  issues, 43, 46; on progress, 105; on role
  of women, 120, 121, 123–24, 132–33;
  support of women's suffrage by, 58,
  136; theology of, 30, 34
—participation of, in church affairs: at
  church conferences, 78, 87, 90, 126; in
  merger of home and foreign mission so-

cieties, 126, 127, 128, 129, 130; in
  movement for Methodist deaconesses,
  62; in Woman's Missionary Council,
  26, 27; in women's laity rights campaign, 131, 138, 139
Bethlehem (Tenn.), 8
Bethlehem Centers, 57, 86, 87, 113
Bible: and role of women in church and
  society, 122–23, 124, 131, 132, 133, 141
Bigotry, religious: among MEC,S women,
  67–68, 69, 70, 72, 144, 145
Biloxi (Miss.), 64
Birmingham: meetings in, 98, 126; mission work in, 87
Birth of a Nation, The, 99
Bivin, George D., 43–44
Blacks: community support of missions
  for, 86; funding of missions for, 87;
  idea of progress for, 101; mission work
  among, 8, 8n, 10, 39, 49, 64, 83,
  84–118 *passim*, 145; mission work by,
  85, 87, 88, 101, 102, 113, 114; opposition to missions for, 147; MEC,S
  women's attitude toward, 107, 108. *See
  also* Race relations, as home mission
  project
Boeckel, Florence, 80
Boykin, Minnie, 64
Brown, Charlotte Hawkins, 89, 90, 91
Brown, O. E., 67
Byrd, Reverend C. W., 18

Capitalism, 1, 51–52, 54, 54n
Carter, Paul, 1, 45n
Catholic Legion of Decency, 44
Chapman, Mrs. J. E., 29
Chappell, Mrs. E. B., 25
Chattanooga, 87
Child labor laws: MEC,S women's inter-
  est in, 41, 41n, 42, 43, 47, 48, 52, 54,
  56, 144

Children: mission work with, 6, 10, 12,
38–39, 41, 43–44, 55–56, 144
China: missionaries in, 8, 9, 10
Christianity: MEC,S women and ideals
of, 20–23, 23n, 24, 26, 28, 28n, 29,
30, 33–35
Cincinnati, 7
City mission work: beginning of, 12–13;
importance of, 65, 67; objects of, 39,
50, 70, 75–76; scope of, 13–14; men-
tioned, 16. *See also* Blacks; Children;
Immigrants
Civil War, 8, 9, 10, 28n
Coal mines, 53
Cobb, Mrs. J. B., 126, 128, 129
Cole, Mrs. E. W., 48
College of Industrial Arts (Denton,
Tex.), 40
College of William and Mary, 40
Colored Methodist Episcopal Church, 84,
94, 114
Commission on Interracial Cooperation
(CIC), 87, 87n, 88, 89, 89n, 91, 93,
95, 108
Committee on Civil Rights, 97
Community improvement: interracial
programs for, 113–14
Conversion: as goal of home mission
work, 24–25
Cooper, Sarah B., 20–21, 39, 55
Costigan-Wagner Act, 98
Council of Women for Home Missions,
103
Crime: causes of, 56
Curtis-Reed bill, 40

Daily Christian Advocate, 136
Dallas, 61
Day-care centers, 48
Deaconesses: in MEC,S, 62–64, 70,
75–76, 93n
DeBardeleben, Mary, 54, 85–86, 106,
107, 108–109, 122, 124, 147
Denton (Tex.), 40
Disarmament, 80, 81
Divorce, 46, 46–47n, 56
Domestic servants: working conditions of,
49
Downs, Francis, 11n

Downs, Mary Isabelle, 22, 29, 58, 78, 79,
95, 109
Du Bois, W. E. B., 105n

East Central State College (Ada, Okla.),
40
Economic reform: interest of MEC,S
women in, 51–55, 59
Ecumenism: growth of, among MEC,S
women, 68, 72
Education: interest of MEC,S women in,
39–41, 43; of women for mission work,
14–15, 15n, 26, 30, 38, 50, 56, 57,
62, 93, 103, 104
—as home missions project: adult, 12;
kindergarten, 39, 55, 86, 144; of
blacks, 39, 99; of black women for
leadership, 114; of immigrants, 39, 65;
of women, 8, 8n
Education, U.S. Department of, 40
Eighmy, John, 2
Eighteenth Amendment, 45
Ely, Richard, 15
Emory University, 27
Environment: effects of, 1, 4, 31–32,
34–35, 36, 105, 106, 107, 115
Ethics: and social Christianity, 1
Evangelism: and social activism, 26, 27
Evans, Reverend W. F., 133–34

Factory workers: mission work with, 38
Family: interest of MEC,S women in,
36–38, 43, 44, 45, 58, 59
Farish, Hunter, 119
Federal Council of Churches, 33, 91
Federation of Colored Women's Clubs, 91
Feminists, 123
Fisk University, 86, 90, 95, 114
Foreign missions, 3, 6, 7, 8, 9, 11, 15, 16,
19, 68, 71, 83, 85; merger of, with
home mission societies, 118, 125–29
Fund raising: for mission work, 38

Galloway, Bishop Charles, 101
Georgia School for the Blind, 16
Gibson, Maria, 119, 128, 129
Girls' High School (Atlanta), 9
Gladden, Washington, 15, 55, 55n
Glenn, E. M., 136